THE CHALLENGE OF THE FUTURE

Also by A. C. Grayling

THE
CHALLENGE
OF THE FUTURE

What Should We
Keep from Yesterday
as We Rush into
Tomorrow?

A. C. GRAYLING

ONEWORLD

A Oneworld Book

First published by Oneworld Publications Ltd in 2026

Copyright © A. C. Grayling, 2026

ISBN 978-1-83643-307-1
eISBN 978-1-83643-308-8

Typeset by Geethik Technologies
Printed and bound in Great Britain by Clays Ltd, Elcograf S.p.A.

The authorised representative in the EEA is eucomply OU,
Pärnu mnt 139b–14, 11317 Tallinn, Estonia
(email: hello@eucompliancepartner.com / phone: +33757690241)

Oneworld Publications Ltd
10 Bloomsbury Street
London WC1B 3SR
England

Stay up to date with the latest books,
special offers, and exclusive content from
Oneworld with our newsletter

Sign up on our website
oneworld-publications.com

MIX
Paper | Supporting
responsible forestry
FSC® C018072

For Lucy and Prue with love and thanks

CONTENTS

PREFACE

Humankind stands at a radical inflection-point in its history. Almost everyone agrees that this is so, and unlike some widely held views, it is true. The future is a chaos of uncertainties. There are some who go further and say that humanity stands not just at an inflection-point, but at its final point, on the verge of self-destruction.

The latter is not impossible, alas, but two things encourage us to think that we could survive the changes rushing upon us, not least from the new technologies that, in the bewildering rapidity of their development, are currently making the future deeply, and in a number of ways threateningly, unreadable.

The first encouragement is that we are not without agency or a modicum of rationality, and could if we are robust direct these unnervingly rapid changes in ways that reduce their dangers and leverage the benefits they also promise.

The second is that to live without hope of survival is impossible; indeed, to hope for something better than mere survival is a necessity: hope is life, and life is the business of working to make hopes come true.

I thought of calling this book 'Under the Raintree', in allusion to the Brazil Raintree, *Brunfelsia pauciflora*, grown as an ornamental bush in gardens round the world and colloquially known as the 'Yesterday, Today and Tomorrow' bush because its flowers change colour as they mature, starting as purple, then fading through lavender to white. It is a bush that graced the African garden in which I lived as a child, and I admired it greatly; it seems an apt metaphor for discussing the time of drastic uncertainty about *tomorrow* that we live in *today*, and the question of what we can bring from *yesterday* – from the past – into today to help us decide about what values, what aspirations, what lessons, to preserve into tomorrow.

To answer the question about what yesterday can offer today and tomorrow, it is necessary first to survey today's anxieties about tomorrow – and its promises. The promises relate to matters that we would do well to leave behind; there are plenty such. The anxieties concern the less desirable and, in many cases, dangerous possibilities that today's developments suggest – indeed more than suggest, for they seem to be inevitable unless managed. If there is one thought we should cling to, it is that unless we look worst-case scenarios squarely in the face, we will not prepare ourselves sufficiently to avoid or mitigate the worst that tomorrow could bring.

INTRODUCTION

Today we are in an era of rapid technological change and uncertainty. Humankind is faced with the question of what the future will be like – and more burningly: should be like – given so many science-fiction-seeming imponderables:

- AI and its effect on work, life and society, including government, welfare, surveillance and social organisation, policing and control, and kinetic, electronic and autonomous weapons of war;
- the possibility of super-AI/AGI (Artificial *General* Intelligence) escaping human control;
- education, the question whether technology will make us smarter or dumber because we outsource too much of our thinking;
- the effect of AI on creativity and the arts;
- new medical possibilities, life-extension, cloning and genetic modification;
- ageing populations;

- a 'transhumanist' humanity implanted with technology, physically and intellectually enhanced by device–tissue interfaces and prosthetic modifications;
- the already-burgeoning reach of humanity into space and its colonisation, with effects on economy, science, competition and the possibility of conflict;
- new systems of communications and production;
- new forms of interpersonal relationships from digital solitude to replacement of relationships by sex robots and virtual friendships;
- the vulnerability to hacking, cyberwar and other disruptions of the technologies we increasingly and indeed existentially rely upon;
- and by far not least: climate change and its devastating potential consequences.

At the same time there are increasing dangers from geopolitical instability, the rise of authoritarianism with its threat to liberties and the rule of law, conflict and developments in new forms and instruments of war both hot and cold which, as with climate change, threaten to make the foregoing suite of possibilities either irrelevant or destined to go in directions even more dramatic, not to say catastrophic.

These bullet points list or imply the downsides of the changes already under way. There are considerable upsides too; the pressing question is what the balance of outcomes will be – and the lesson of history is that unless they are understood and prepared for, the downsides will have an enhanced tendency to overbalance the upsides, on the same principle as 'bad money drives out good'.

It verges on banality to say that *today* we are in a state of semi-blindness about *tomorrow* because the dizzying developments that rush upon us daily make it hard to see where we are going.

Most people feel passive under the barrage of change. It seems irresistible and out of control. Yet even the most superficial thought about what is happening and what our response should be reveals to us that there is so much that is undesirable about our *yesterday* as a species – only consider our history: what we have done to ourselves, each other and the planet over time – that a temptation to call a halt to current developments, a conservative desire to maintain a status quo, prompts the sceptical response: Really? Do we so value our bad old ways, our conflicts and wars, our greedy economic systems, our destruction of the planet's environment and climate, our hostilities and prejudices, our dental decay, heart disease and cancer, that we wish to preserve ourselves and everything else as they now are?

At the same time, from *yesterday* come some of the best thoughts our species has so far had about what matters in life if it is decoupled from the evils, natural and self-created by humanity, that beset it. What are these values? Do they still persuade, and if so what appeal can be made to them in trying not to be a passive subject – or victim – of the storm of changes flooding over us, but instead to be in control of them: to create the future, not merely to let it happen to us?

This book has two parts – Part I, 'Today and Tomorrow': what is happening today that makes us concerned about tomorrow, and Part II, 'Tomorrow and Yesterday': what we wish to leave behind, what we wish to preserve, what it can teach us about managing today and tomorrow.

Part I surveys the challenges and possibilities both good and bad in the onrush of changes, not least in technology, that are swamping us. From galloping AI developments and their effects on industry, commerce, government, employment, education, war and policing; from interpersonal human relations to political systems; from outer space to tech implants within the human brain and body – the future is bewildering in its likelihoods and possibilities. What is happening today, already, gives rise to a blizzard of hopes and fears, and above all of uncertainty. What are the auguries already promisingly or alarmingly present, now, in this period of rapid transition? Do any of them hold out better hopes, if we can survive the threats that other developments pose or seem to pose? What are the current facts about what AI can and cannot do, about population growth or decline, about the social trends already introduced by the digitisation of so many aspects of life? Already mass surveillance face-recognition technology is in use in China and almost every major airport in the world; electronic communications and social media are routinely trawled and monitored by security agencies; new generations of remote and autonomous weapons are at work on battlefields; lunar orbital space stations for commercial operations and colonisation of space are in advanced planning stages; genetic engineering using

CRISPR technology is already possible, as is gene-modification therapy; *today* we already live in circumstances that are dramatically different from the past, and yet these developments are only at an early stage.

One area of debate is transhumanism ('transhumans' are human beings who are a combination of technology with the human body and brain). Possibilities in this arena involve medical science, interpersonal relationships, human capacities across a wide range from sports to 'super-soldiers' and brain-enhancements that potentiate intellectual powers. Life-extension as well as physical and neurological enhancement is on the cards. For example: the research arms of the US, Chinese and other militaries (see the US's published DARPA suite of projects) are seeking to produce super-soldiers impervious to pain and the need for sleep, with battlefield technology for vision, communications and data implanted rather than carried outside the body on helmets and body-armour – yet even as large sums are spent on research into these possibilities, war technology is already moving in the direction of largely or wholly machine warfare, drones, robots and autonomous weapons systems. Reproductive technologies aimed at gestating human infants outside the human body to avoid the limitations and pains of childbirth are being researched, with major consequences for the nature of interpersonal relationships. Direct inputs via brain–chip implants – already in use for control of certain neurological complaints – suggest a range of possibilities from education to policing, emotional control, memory manipulation and direct 'thought to thought' communication. Extension of the human lifespan and the effects on economies and demographics are already under vigorous discussion. None of these are science fiction; they are in reach, or already here.

Thinking about technology, AI and transhumanism constitutes the chief focus in the burgeoning discipline of future studies, in popular parlance known as 'futurology', a self-explanatory name. There are futurist institutes and research centres (some at leading universities such as Oxford, Edinburgh and Toronto) where serious study is devoted to prognostication. Some of what such studies outline is eutopian,[1] some dystopian; almost all paint pictures that are radically different from what we are accustomed to. Among the dystopian possibilities a significant one is the collapse – under the weight of what can be triggered by developing technologies, climate change, population growth or decline and weapons of mass destruction – back into primitive-technology conditions, in effect to an Iron Age or Stone Age situation. Futurists have been around for some time, and past futurists made prognostications about futures that are already in our past – one could ask how their prophecies fared, to which the answer is generally: not always very well – and that gives pause, because much of what is to be discussed in the first part of this book consists in futurist thinking. But what is the alternative?

Looming over all is the climate change challenge. It could, as already remarked, make other anxieties about the future irrelevant, on the unimpeachable ground that there might be no future.

The second part surveys the bad things about history and the human condition we would do well to escape, and – more to the point; and far more importantly – asks what good things we risk losing. Above all, it asks whether there are permanent values that are worth preserving, and if so, how they can survive the transition to a world where the conditions for the expression of those values might no longer exist, or in which they are severely complicated and compromised by new conditions and demands; or whether these demands will require abandonment of aspirations once cherished as fundamental to human flourishing. We think of human rights, justice, education, love, friendship, the family, co-operation and peace; why did they recommend themselves in the first place, what role have they played in the human story, and how much weight should we give them in light of the fact that so much of history has been a narrative of conflict, oppressions, injustice and suffering, suggesting that these values seem not to have protected us very well in the past? Do we need new values – and will the onrushing changes affecting human nature and society offer or demand new and different values? What might they be?

As it happens, among the possible scenarios surveyed in Part I, some preserve some of the values once and now thought most important; others project a need for – or the inevitability of – new and different values. If the former is the case, what hopes are hinted at? If the latter, the radical disjunction between humanity and society as it has been and as it will be is radical indeed. The former would be a continuation, and perhaps the fuller application, of the values mentioned: human rights, justice, love, friendship, the family, co-operation and peace. If the latter involves an abandonment of some or all of these things, what does that say about the future of humanity? Would one wish to be part of it?

The fundamental point at issue is, *What really matters to being human, what really matters for the possibility of good societies,* and the confronting question is: will future humans, will future societies, no longer be 'human' or 'social' in any sense that would keep this fundamental point relevant? And if so, would it matter?

In sum: we are at an unprecedented crossroads *today* between *yesterday* and *tomorrow.* How are we to decide what path or paths we should – or can – take; indeed is there any 'can' about it, or has the path already been taken for us by the fact that we have been and are so far behind the curve of change? And if so, is there a way back to the crossroads where a different choice of path can be made?

Such a forest of questions! At least some of the answers are suggested in the pages to come.

PART I

TODAY AND TOMORROW

1

'ARTIFICIAL' 'INTELLIGENCE'

One way to dramatise to ourselves our uncertainties about the future is to ask such questions as the following. Driverless cars are already on our streets, driverless trains are already running on rail networks; what do we think about pilotless airplanes? Wouldn't we welcome a technology that places sensors on our bodies, diagnoses any conditions afflicting it, and prescribes (and may even carry out) procedures specifically tailored to our individual genetic makeup and current physical status? What if the government of our country were an AI that crunched all the national economic and sociological data and legislated what to do next? Might we prefer to have future wars, if there have to be any, fought between drones and robots, not people? As to AI-powered robots: is not a world desirable in which no one does housework, no one is lonely, no one is living without sex, because everyone has personal spouse-robots who do and provide everything in these ways, and do it with a more-than-plausible appearance of kindness, sensitivity, co-operation and responsiveness?

What about flipping a switch to have an AI-written e-book tailored to one's tastes, or a film or television series created in accordance with one's prompts, with actors (or their indistinguishable avatars) of one's choice, instantly available? What indeed if all books, paintings, music, television dramas, news broadcasts, were AI produced and delivered on demand?

How about an AI kitchen with a device in it – let's call it a 'multicuisinier' – into which one decants a bag of the basic chemicals out of which plant and animal matter is (or was previously) made, and which, upon a few presses of its keyboard, produces delicious lunches and dinners, glasses of wine, etc., all nutritious but devoid of harmful substances (e.g. saturated fat, salt and sugar, all absent but their taste perfectly and safely mimicked)?

How about a closet into which you step, on getting out of bed, which showers you, passing currents through you to stimulate muscles as exercise would, then dries and clothes you, as it does so activating the cuisinier in the kitchen so that your coffee and breakfast await you when you step out of the closet; and as you take your cup and plate from the cuisinier it alerts a driverless taxi to be at your door in so-many minutes, knowing your routine? Indeed your toilet might, upon analysing your voidings, instruct you to plug into a physician-machine on the way home from work – indeed, might already tell you what is wrong if anything is – and perhaps estimate the approximate date of your death.

All right: I am waxing fanciful here (or – how fanciful, I wonder?). But it was not much less than a decade before this writing that a friend of mine, after making an appointment online with a clinic in Manhattan, began to receive advertisements for a local funeral parlour, because the algorithm that directed the ads to him knew ('knew') a number of things that made it think ('think') he would find the ads useful, viz. what the clinic specialised in, his age, how often he had been there before, what sort of food and drink he ordered online ... all in all, getting the ads gave him an unpleasant start, because its actuarial bluntness contrasted with his physician's soothing evasions. I repeat: that was *some years* ago. In the advance of the technologies involved, things have already moved ahead by centuries.

The scenarios just painted all involve AI, and AI is the chief game-changer in so much of what is happening that discussing it cannot be avoided.

Human intelligence has ever applied itself to making tools and outsourcing labour to them. From the first chipped flints to AI systems, the story is fundamentally the same. So too is the fact that some of the tools made by humans have made humans smarter, increasing their capacities, and some have made them dumber, diminishing their capacities. The development of increasingly sophisticated tools required specialisation because of the expertise needed to make and wield them, this being one of the principal factors in the development of complex societies requiring media of exchange between different specialists, given that the presence of specialists obviates the need for others to acquire the specialism – thus losing the capacity to do for themselves what they can get by trading or buying. For example, very few now could make a refrigerator for themselves, at least beyond the crudest of devices for chilling and therefore keeping foodstuffs edible for longer.

Some tools change things hugely. The automobile has transformed cities and the way people live in them, for a major example. An aerial view of a large city shows what a stranglehold its roads have on it. Like poisonous serpents, the major roads leading into and across cities blight what is around the greater part of their routes; look at the space beneath a flyover interchange – a wasteland; look at the sterile high-rise car-parks, the blocked veins of minor streets along which, between the rows of parked vehicles, other cars and buses squeeze their way. The noise and pollution reach hideous levels – but the convenience trumps all. Another tool – the bomb – shows how convenient a road system is by showing how inconvenient it is to have it disrupted.

All tools develop from simpler forms of themselves, and meet needs people have or imagine they have. The automobile developed from the horse and carriage as 'the horseless carriage' ('car', obviously, is an abbreviation of 'carriage'), thus making horses redundant, depriving people of horse-dung – fuel for burning, manure for vegetable gardens – and giving them in return faster, further and soon more comfortable travel at additional costs: of noise, pollution, the geopolitical consequences of oil hunger. Likewise the bullet, the bomb, the missile, are developments from the arrow and the catapult, the spear and the sword. Clever of us, though unwise.

From the abacus to the computer and thence the extremely fast powerful systems we call AI the trajectory is the same. Many of the innovations that recommended themselves as really superb developments of preceding technology were almost instantaneous in their take-up and spread. The movable type printing press invented by Johannes Gutenberg in the 1440s produced its first book in 1450; by fifty years later nine million books had been printed all over Europe, transforming the continent's culture irreversibly. Mobile telephones looked clunky – weighing two kilograms, and the size of a brick – with little network reach on first appearing in the 1970s, but by the early 1990s second-generation ('2G') digital cellular networks and miniaturisation of phone components saw an enormous surge in take-up of the technology. The packet-switching advance in 3G technology introduced in 2001 turned the mobile phone into the 'smartphone'; no longer just a phone but, very soon, an internet terminal.

Mobile phones developed from radio-telephones ('RT') as used by the military in the Second World War, though with a bit of a stretch one could say that telephone boxes, like the iconic red telephone boxes in British towns, were a form of mobile telephone, their users being the 'mobile' part of the arrangement. Each stage in the development of a technology is embryonic in its preceding stage, achieving more effectively and quickly the aim for which the original technology was itself developed. The mobile phone is a descendant of the hill-top beacon, the semaphore flags on sailing ships, the telegraph.

Some developments take 'quantum leaps' by combining several hitherto different technologies, each leveraging the other. The smartphone is an example; getting the internet on your phone's screen required making your phone a mini-computer and connecting it to the web. The phone can reach out to another individual phone, person-to-person, which is what telephones were built to do, but it can also reach out to the entire universe of the web. A common source of wonder is that the computing power in a contemporary (at time of writing) mobile phone is vastly greater than on the moon-landing Apollo 11 in 1969: over 100,000 times the processing power, more than a million times the Random Access Memory, and more than seven million times the Read Only Memory.

The rate of development in computing and AI technology has accelerated ever faster. By the middle of the second decade of the twenty-first century AI was everywhere, mainly in the form of 'narrow AI' ('expert systems') dedicated to specific tasks in industry and commerce, such as monitoring the performance of equipment and governing its functioning in factories, adjusting electricity supply to demand, matching retail goods supply to demand, choosing routes in traffic, analysing financial data and making rapid trades on tiny fluctuations in stock market prices, indeed forecasting movement in all kinds of markets; it guides missiles, helps to design and fly aircraft and to assist air traffic control, analyses patient data in medical settings and helps to design new drugs – one could go on and on across many fields. And in most of them AI is a powerful adjunct to our species' capabilities.

During this rapid unfolding of AI in so many domains voices were raised in concern about future possibilities relating to AI and especially 'AGI' – 'Artificial General Intelligence'

– with superhuman-type intelligence and the possibility of harm to humanity if it escapes human control. This concern was raised very early, even before the term 'AI' itself was coined in the mid-1950s. In 1949 the 'father of cybernetics', Norbert Wiener, wrote, 'We had better be quite sure that the purpose we put into the machine is the purpose which we really desire'.[1] For several decades thereafter the faltering and uncertain development of early AI made such anxieties marginal; most people were sceptical about the prospect of *artificial* intelligence ever matching *real, human* intelligence, let alone surpassing it. But by the second decade of the twenty-first century that sentiment had changed dramatically, and alarmed voices were raised. Nick Bostrom and Eliezer Yudkowsky – the latter had in fact already mooted the possibility of AI threatening humanity in his 'Paperclip' thought-experiment of 2003 (an AI governing paperclip manufacture goes wrong and turns everything, including humans, into paperclips) – were warning that the growing possibility of AGI presents an existential threat to humanity if misaligned with human interests.[2] Bostrom's book *Superintelligence* was published in 2014; shortly thereafter major figures in science and computing, among them Bill Gates, Stephen Hawking, Demis Hassabis, Stuart Russell, Max Tegmark and Elon Musk, issued similar warnings about AI, in 2015 signing with others the Future of Life Institute's 'Open Letter' on AI-driven autonomous weapons systems ('killer robots').[3]

On the very day the words before you were written, a *Wall Street Journal* article quoted another concerned AI expert,

Mustafa Suleyman, saying, 'We want to create types of systems that are aligned to human values by default. That means they are not designed to exceed and escape human control.'[4] That aspiration is one that the unpredictability and indeed mystery – for so it is: because what is going on inside the latest AI systems is not fully understood – renders more acute. The 'latest' systems at time of writing are those that flow from the game-changer moment in 2017 when 'deep learning' was combined with natural language processing, by means of a new design for large language models (LLMs) known as 'transformer architecture'. The announcement of ChatGPT in November 2022 was the moment at which the arrival of 'generative AI' reached public consciousness. The explosion of LLM systems that followed has moved with light-speed. There were chatbots before – we had all grown frustratedly familiar with the 'customer help' systems that guard the gates to businesses and services we try to interact with when we have queries, complaints and needs; now, at time of writing, multi-modal chat systems are 'agentic' – can do things like book your tickets, write your emails, serve as 'copilots' in all your tasks and those of businesses, lawyers, doctors, politicians, military commanders – and appear so human-like in interactions with users that people become emotionally dependent on them.

These developments magnify the risks that the warning voices had already identified. There are many. There are no systematic controls over what AI does, although different AI companies say that they build in monitoring systems to combat bias, misinformation, errors, fraud and security breaches – yet all these are frequently detected. AIs that calculate mortgage applicant risks have been seen to discriminate against people of colour. Medical misdiagnoses, deepfakes, 'hallucinations' (false information), the use of AI by hackers and scammers, and much more – but above all the possibility of losing control of AI that can teach itself, improve its capacities on its own, and take directions that 'misalign' with human interests – are open-ended to the point of being existential for humanity. The notion that AI might be 'humanity's last invention' is no longer fanciful. Without doubt the current deficiencies of AI will quickly be improved upon; it is a mistake to think that 'there are some things AI will never be able to do'. But that includes deciding ('deciding') to do things, or just doing things, 'misaligned with human interests'. In this way, the existential risk problem is of a different order from the other, remediable, problems already familiar and likely to be corrected.

The point is dramatised in an interview given by Jared Kaplan of Anthropic, the AI company he co-owns, at the end of 2025. In it he says that humankind will soon be faced with deciding whether to let AI systems autonomously train themselves and design their successor systems, which will have one of two outcomes: either a huge 'intelligence explosion' or loss of control by human beings.[5] He describes this decision as 'extremely high-stakes' and the biggest humanity will ever make. So far AI companies have tried to ensure that the alignment sought by Bostrom, Suleyman and others is maintained, but 'letting AI go' to self-improve recursively marks the end of that endeavour. His colleague at Anthropic, Jack Clark, said in

October 2025 that he was both optimistic and yet 'deeply afraid' about AI because it is 'a real and mysterious creature, not a simple and predictable machine'.[6] Kaplan says the questions are:

> Do you lose control over it? Do you even know what AIs are doing? Are the AIs good for humanity? Are they helpful? Are they going to be harmless? Do they understand people? Are they going to allow people to continue to have agency over their lives and over the world? ... [it would be] very dangerous if it fell into the wrong hands ... I think preventing power grabs – preventing misuse of the technology – is also very important.[7]

A problem with the control and alignment question is that AI companies are in a race with each other to develop ever more powerful systems – OpenAI, Google DeepMind, Meta, xAI, China's DeepSeek, are all trying to get to the front, exponentially driven by considerations of 'investment, revenue, capabilities of AI, how complex the tasks [that] AI can do'.[8] One marker of the race is that 'research into frontier AI models, including ChatGPT, shows the length of tasks AIs can do has been doubling every seven months'.[9] Already AI is on the way to being able to do 'most white-collar work' before 2030, and Kaplan adds that it is already the case that 'his six-year-old son will never be better than an AI at academic work such as writing an essay or doing a maths exam'.[10]

If AI were to escape human control and wipe out humanity, and is on course to acquiring the capacity to do so, discussions such as this might already be unnecessary because too late.

'Too late' is the saddest phrase in the language. But on the principle that hope must never be abandoned, one must consider the better possibility of fulfilment of all the benign and neutral promises of AI, and ask what humanity's future will be like in light of them.

The enhancement of human activities in almost all spheres has already been vastly achieved by AI. One promise is that all the drudgery can be removed from life – all the repetitive, low-level, boring, dangerous, dirty work – leaving people freer to enjoy the avocations of leisure, creativity and human interaction. This is not eutopian; it really could happen. But even this best-case scenario – the idea that economic activity and wealth-generation is performed by AI systems such that most people are permanently at leisure, with national wealth being distributed through some form of national wage scheme – provokes a reaction from those who think this a rebarbative idea; for where is aspiration, striving, challenge, the personal growth that meeting challenges brings; where is ambition, where is the grist that difficulties bring to the mill, making life purposive?

Well: a reset in what counts as things worth doing and being, a set of goals that are about different values than what money measures (income, the size and location of your house, the marque of your car, the things only accessible through success in money-terms), would be required, and formal and informal education, the latter achieved through the conversation society has with itself about what is good and what – when success by this metric is attained – confers status, could shift our gaze in that direction. This too seems eutopian, at least for the transitional interim, and perhaps it is. But in a world where no one *has* to work to pay for the endless bureaucracy of being alive – taxes, mortgages, rent, bills, tickets, insurance, food, clothing, transport, holidays, and the rest – might such a reset be possible? It is not as if humankind has not been there before; in fact, life as we live it in the 9a.m.-to-5p.m. bills-to-pay world is a recent phenomenon, a form of serfdom in economic arrangements that has evolved over the last few centuries under the pressure of the agrarian and industrial revolutions and the post-industrial age. Before then life had different patterns, seasonal, rotating periods of intense labour with periods of leisure, time a matter of months not minutes, most labour far more under individual control even when done at the bidding of other people and other forces.

These thoughts relate to the possibility, indeed probability, that AI will displace many occupations and jobs. It has been pointed out that in 1865, at the end of the Civil War in the US, over half the population was engaged in agriculture, but by 1950 this figure had dropped to 15%, because of mechanisation.[11] The shift was absorbed by the territorial spread of the US (appropriating Native American lands) and the effects of the 'Frontier' described by Frederick Jackson Turner,[12] alongside a rapid burgeoning of industry with a concomitant growth of cities, further promoted, until 1920, by an immense amount of encouraged immigration. Well and good; the shift to industry absorbed the numbers displaced from agriculture. Compare horses: in 1865 horses (and mules) were essential to agriculture in the US, but by 1950 they had been displaced by tractors.[13] In the AI take-over of tasks and roles, are we people or horses? If people are redundant to much of the economic process, what will absorb their energies?

Answering that question by looking backwards and around rather than ahead, in doing the latter asking what so-far unimagined possibilities there might be for human energies and ambitions, is the first mistake. There is a tendency to take today's ways, and then think of ourselves as unemployed in them. That misleads us. LLMs might be or come to be imaginative, but we humans still are; this is where imagination has to come fully into play.

One type of scenario is AI-assisted personalised learning of all sorts of interesting things, for example of languages or other diverse skills, of immersive virtual travel that supplements and informs real-time real-world travel, enhanced because we are AI-facilitated in many of the ways that make such activities easier and more enjoyable – healthier, better informed, better equipped all round to take advantage of them. The health point is not trivial; AI in healthcare, focused on one's genetics and optimal ways of preventing or managing physical disease and mental unease, already has the potential to reduce suffering and improve the quality and probably the quantity of life.

Meanwhile AI-aided management of problems ranging from climate change impacts and natural disasters to geopolitical tensions, conflicts and diplomacy might improve the global situation. Information and the reasoning required to analyse, predict and decide what to do on the basis of that information is already a commonplace of AI assistance in human affairs, and as the exponential increase of power and capability of AI continues, with glitches and flaws progressively reduced, improvement in this respect is a legitimate hope.

What is needed for the benign, the positive, the at-least neutral, influence of AI? The consensus is that at the minimum AI has to be constrained to align with human interests – so: these need to be identified and agreed, clarity and consensus being vital – which most fundamentally involves ensuring that the data on which AI systems are trained is fully diverse, its outputs robustly audited for bias and error with corrections constantly made (the functionality for which ought to be embodied within systems themselves). Access to AI has to be universal and equitable, with everyone as adept at utilising it as most people today are adept at using their smartphones.

All this said, the thought remains that the ultimate existential risk cannot be 100% guarded against. It would take only one suicidal bad-actor computer genius to intervene in a way that skews some global AI system to humanity-destructive ends. There are plenty of bad actors out there; again at time of writing, AI companies are dealing with a new threat – attackers weaponising AI against itself. There is a new challenge posed by malware strains that infect and rewrite code, viruses that mutate rapidly to escape detection and improve themselves. A mutating, self-developing malware virus, given the intentions with which it was injected into a system to disrupt and/or control it, could not only harm its target but escape and get into the AI environment more widely.

Worse than bad actors and more to the present point – this being the concern in all those warning voices – AI itself could go wrong, or take a wrong turning, whether or not intentionally (though the question of intentionality and consciousness in AI systems is moot), and its sheer power at protecting itself and outmanoeuvring efforts at intervention or control, by means of its far superior intelligence, would doom us ineluctably.

This is why the Future of Life Institute (FLI), jointly with Encode Justice, issued its stark Open Letter of October 2025, signed among hundreds of others by Geoffrey Hinton, Steve Wozniak, Yoshua Bengio, a variety of celebrities and public figures including an adviser to the Pope, even a serving staff member of OpenAI, stating, 'We call for a prohibition on the development of superintelligence, not lifted before there is broad scientific consensus that it will be done safely and controllably, and [with] strong public buy-in.'[14]

This is a call for far more robust action than taken by the EU, whose AI Act of 2024 is the world's first major risk-based initiative for managing general-purpose 'strong AI' systems.[15] The EU Act calls for AI used in Europe to be 'safe, transparent, traceable, non-discriminatory and environmentally friendly'.[16] The FLI call is for much more: for a *ban*, albeit temporary, on any future development of strong AI until there is a governance framework, democratically constituted, ensuring its safety and controllability. The vital question of what form that framework should take and how control should be exercised was left open. The addressee of the Open Letter was the US government, though it urged the US government to take a lead in setting international standards and regulatory consensus because 'AI harms are borderless'. And it insisted that 'industry voices' should not dominate the agenda, but instead that there must be input from 'civil society, academia and the public'.[17]

Eminently worthy though this call is, in Donald Trump's America, with its mega-rich 'tech-bros' calling the shots, *regulation* is the least likely thing to happen.

FLI's call for a ban on further development addresses the most dramatic risks that AI could pose, threatening either the end of humanity or, only somewhat less dismal from humanity's point of view, the end of civilisation. (The rest of the animate and inanimate world might regard neither as a catastrophe.) But there are other sub-existential risks that also require investigation.

AI malfunction or misdirection could do great harm less than total catastrophe, yet adversely affecting millions or tens of millions of people. An example would be disruption of energy supply, transport, the internet, or control of air traffic, or the triggering of wars caused by false information reaching a government already apprehensive about a neighbouring state's intentions. Likewise the failure or misdirection of AI, whether caused by itself or an outside agency, could cause such disruption of financial markets that economic collapse greater than experienced in 2008 could occur, with all the deleterious effects involved.

AI can be used – indeed, is already being used – to surveil and manipulate people. Authoritarian regimes find this a godsend. Gaslighting whole populations is facilitated by AI generation of misinformation and tendentious messaging; AI directs people down social media rabbit-holes that reinforce prejudices and inflame hostility against those perceived as a threat – immigrants, the opposition political party: this is par for the course in Trump's US. By the same token societies can be destabilised by the same means, stoking disaffection and portraying affairs as dangerous to groups whose interests already feel under siege. By its nature surveillance is an invasion of privacy, and is not restricted to government policing; commercial interests monitor people's behaviour, choices and proclivities in the interest of maximising profits, and it is private tech companies which provide them with the wherewithal to do it.

A major threat in this respect is the way that AI-generated misinformation and AI-stoked disaffection can undermine democracy. Given that democracy, for all its imperfections, generally protects significant degrees of individual liberties and the rule of law, this is serious. A detailed discussion of this matter occurs in my *For the People*.[18]

Think again about AI's displacement of human labour. In his *A World Without Work*, Daniel Susskind distinguishes two kinds of unemployment: 'frictional' and 'structural'.[19] In the first kind jobs are replaced by AI systems (think driverless trucks) and might even create new jobs (in software engineering, say), but not all middle-aged truck drivers will be able to take software engineering jobs. In the second kind, AI displacement of roles might result in there being *no* jobs available. At very least in the transition to a new world of enforced leisure (unemployment) there will be difficult adjustments required to thinking about purpose, self-esteem and meaning, and even to patterns of family life and personal behaviour. An allied and equally serious consideration is that in a situation where AI does everything and people are recalibrating the purpose of life away from work and its ambitions, the small number of *owners* of AI systems, such as Meta, Google, Apple and Amazon, will be in positions of vast power. The world is already wracked by enormous disparities in wealth – some live in circumstances of conspicuous luxury, others sleep on the streets in all weathers, most have to count their pennies – so even if a condition of economic abundance allows for a national wage to be paid, the disparities can only grow larger.

A particularly dismaying thought is that in the leisured/ unemployed society people will spend yet more time gazing at the screens of their smartphones and laptops, among them those who anonymously vomit into them their prejudices, hatreds, resentments and antipathies, their abuse and their lies, their bullying, defamation and threats. Some even now do this as their full-time occupation; their being joined by millions more is an ugly prospect. The harm caused by this activity, not least to children, which extends to people committing suicide or being driven to acts of violence, is already a datum. The thought of it ballooning further turns one's stomach.[20]

All these negatives share another: that running the technology on which AI systems rely consumes huge amounts of energy – the internet uses up to 536 terawatt-hours of electricity annually (2025 figure).[21] That number is not set to reduce; on the contrary. In itself this is not a problem if the energy comes from renewable sources. But into the foreseeable future this, as an added demand on the world's energy systems, is a contributor to global warming. AI data centres in the US are so power-hungry that they have driven up electricity bills, a fact that played into Democrat election victories in Virginia, Georgia and elsewhere in November 2025. The *New Republic* reported that 'data center opposition is remarkably bipartisan. A large proportion of Big Tech's AI infrastructure buildout is occurring in red states, like Indiana, Texas, Ohio, and West Virginia, where data centers have added billions of dollars to household energy bills and inspired serious hostility from Democrats and Republicans alike.'[22]

Even if one dials down further from the risks and threats of these sub-existential levels, there are concerns about AI. Until AI systems are perfect, without error, 'hallucinations', algorithmic bias or unreliability of performance, the fact that so many functions rely on them introduces risk. You might be charged too much for your insurance premium, or denied a visa, or given incorrect medical test results, or not be invited to a job interview, or accused of a crime you did not commit, because of a glitch in an AI system. Such things happen. AI is spreading through health and justice systems, education and finance, militaries and government departments. It helps greatly; no question. But it is not yet perfect and may never be; there's the concern, given the importance of what happens in these fields.

The key point, however, is that the most serious anxieties – the existential ones – are real. AI could do harm even without 'meaning' to; in the intrinsic nature of a system that develops its own capacities and by their means its own priorities and goals, there could emerge radical conflict with human interests. In the vast amount of data on which such systems train themselves there are many ugly things – the speeches of Hitler, the actions of Genghis Khan who made pyramids out of the skulls of entire city populations he slaughtered, the DNA of plague bacteria, plus the ease with which an AI could learn how to hack into a nuclear weapons system and take control of it – and with unimpeachable logic could draw inferences from the accumulation of such data about how to expunge what is indeed the actual greatest threat both to the planet and to its own existence, viz. human beings. What is the level of probability that this could happen?

Evidently, the dire assessment of all those who have signed successive Open Letters from FLI is that it is not less than 50%.

Well: to revert to the more hopeful idea that AI might prove to be benign or neutral in its swiftly burgeoning effects on us, the question presses: with what do we wish it to be 'aligned' in human interests? That is the subject of Part II. One way of formulating the question is to ask: Suppose a super-AGI conceived of itself on the model of a loving deity keen to protect and enhance human flourishing. What would it do? On the matter of what it thinks is best for human beings turns the answer to be sought in Part II. But one could let fancy have wings for a moment, and wonder whether, on inspection of the inequalities and injustices in the world, Mother Goddess AI would hack into the global financial system and redistribute the money equally to all bank accounts, would release from prisons all those incarcerated for man-made laws premised on moralistic conceptions of the right and the good, send robocops to arrest Putin and Donald Trump, start drying up the oil wells and accelerating by centuries the provision of safe clean energy technologies, provide the recipes for drugs that end communicable diseases, delete misinformation on the internet, reveal the identity of all social media users thus ending the scourge of anonymity from behind the veil of which so much poison spews, and open the secret discussions of politicians to public view. All this would be interesting. Some (the owners of the big bank accounts, politicians) would not see a Mother Goddess AI as benign at all.

2

FUTURES AND FUTURE PEOPLE

Speculation about the future permeates the preceding chapter specifically in relation to the effect of AI. A broader view takes in other factors. The formal discipline of 'future studies' is not confined to academic institutions only, but is in the genome of think-tanks, commercial companies, government departments and the military. It is a serious enterprise which seeks to infer future possibilities from current trends and their histories. It is not entirely or even largely dispassionate; indeed it typically embodies normative judgements – judgements about what best actions to take given how things are trending. 'What *should* be done?' is the question that immediately follows upon 'What is likely?' and 'What could be done?' By gathering considerations from a variety of historical, technological, sociological, economic, political and philosophical sources it seeks to portray with as high a degree of probability as possible where things are going in some respect, how they might turn out, which among them are more likely – and, in line with the normative aspect, which would be preferable. Future studies practitioners warn against thinking that 'The Future' is a single comprehensive monolithic entity, choosing instead to think in terms of alternative scenarios, and in particular of these in connection with specific subject-matters.

Someone once said that 'prediction, especially about the future, is a mug's game', and although that is not wholly true, it reminds us that in the earliest days of heavier-than-air flight people thought that biplanes flew better than monoplanes, and therefore predicted that future aircraft would have twelve wings. Conscious of the risks, serious futurists do not often attempt precise predictions, but quantification of alternative probabilities. Businesses, governments and other agencies find these indispensable for planning. It would be irrational not to, even though 'black swans' – unforeseeable, accidental, wholly adventitious events – often enough fly in to upend the best-laid plans.

The methods available to futurists are various and used in combination. One is to study what happened with past processes and trends; a second is to feed current data into a computer and let it run a variety of extrapolations; a third is to gather and evaluate different expert views about the onward course of trends. Modelling of possible scenarios consists in inferences from analysis of this data, crunching statistics to do it. Among the big questions about where current trends are going are the impact of AI on society, the possibilities suggested by expansion of knowledge and technical capacity in genetic science and health, the associated problems of population growth and all that it implies (including urbanisation, migration, energy needs, food security), the future of what happens in space, and not least the impacts of climate change. These are all linked, because their direct effect on economic factors flows straight through to social and political concerns.

A survey of some of the thinking about future scenarios in three further key areas – human beings themselves, the exploitation of resources in space, and the climate – provides much food for thought. Take each in turn, beginning in this chapter with 'transhumanism'.

The combination of biotechnology, nanotechnology and AI seems to some thinkers to promise a new evolutionary stage for humanity: the 'transhuman' stage. Transhumanism envisages a situation in which positive human capacities are enhanced by combining humans with technologies, whether external to their bodies, modified by them, or implanted in them, at the same time eliminating factors that hamper and degrade human capabilities, among them disease and the abbreviated lifespan that people typically find undesirable. The term 'transhumanism' was coined by Julian Huxley in 1957 as the title for an essay in his collection *New Bottles for New Wine*.[1] He wrote:

> The new understanding of the universe has come about through new knowledge amassed in the last hundred years – by psychologists, biologists, and other scientists, by archaeologists, anthropologists, and historians. It has defined man's responsibility and destiny to be an agent for the rest of the world in the job of realising its inherent potentialities as fully as possible.

It is as if man had been suddenly appointed managing director of the biggest business of all, the business of evolution – appointed without being asked if he wanted it, and without proper warning and preparation. What is more, he can't refuse the job. Whether he wants to or not, whether he is conscious of what he is doing or not, he *is* in point of fact determining the future direction of evolution on this earth. That is his inescapable destiny, and the sooner he realises it and starts believing in it, the better for all concerned.

What the job really boils down to is this – the fullest realization of man's possibilities, whether by the individual, by the community, or by the species in its processional adventure along the corridors of time.[2]

He goes on to say that the exploration of human potential, unlike exploration of the uninhabited parts of the world, had scarcely begun in his day.

We need to explore and map the whole realm of human possibility, as the realm of physical geography has been explored and mapped. How to create new possibilities for ordinary living? What can be done to bring out the latent capacities of the ordinary man and woman for understanding and enjoyment … We are beginning to realize that even the most fortunate people are living far below capacity.[3]

And he acknowledges that bringing out these capacities will transform society: 'This process ... will begin by destroying the ideas and the institutions that stand in the way of our realizing our possibilities (or even deny that the possibilities are there to be realized), and will go on by at least making a start with the actual construction of true human destiny.'[4]

Even though Huxley was a biologist, he did not conceive of this transformation as being effected by biotechnological or technological means. And he was not a eugenicist in the negative sense of one who seeks to improve the human stock by exterminating 'undesirables' in order to prevent them passing on their imperfections to future generations.[5] He was instead a euthenicist, one who believes that by improving the *conditions* of human life, human beings themselves will be improved. His two positive suggestions were that action should be taken to ensure that people live in beautiful surroundings (which meant getting rid of ugly and depressing towns, which he condemned as 'immoral'), and to limit population growth. In a later essay in the same volume he identifies *ideas* as the vectors of human evolution – memes not genes, as we now say – though he grants that future biological science, which includes medicine, might play a role too.[6]

Though Huxley coined the term, the impulses behind transhumanism have existed since earliest recorded history. The alchemists of the Renaissance seeking the elixir of youth were recapitulating Gilgamesh's search for immortality as recounted in the epic that bears his name, dating from over four thousand years ago.[7] All religions with beliefs in an afterlife are a version, some with bodily survival or resurrection and some with a disembodied, altered form of existence. The burial practices of ancient Egyptians and other peoples before them, in which the dead are provided with wherewithal for continued existence, demonstrate the same hope. Wilde's *Dorian Gray* lies in the margins of this genre of thinking. These are just a few examples of thought about transformed human existence; references to tropes in Dante, utopian writings from all periods, even suggestions in the philosophies of Descartes and Nietzsche, demonstrate a widespread desire to overcome humanity's limitations either entirely or in the course of a natural lifetime.[8]

But transhumanism as a cluster of theories since Huxley, though some have defeat of death in their sights, all principally have enhancement of capacity and quality of life as their chief goal, and all turn to the new possibilities provided by biology and technology as the instrument. The person credited with bringing transhumanism into wider notice is 'FM-2030', the name chosen by Fereidoun Esfandiary, a Persian-American professor at the New School in New York, who had represented Iran as an Olympic athlete in basketball and wrestling, was a member of the UN Conciliation Commission on Palestine in the early 1950s, and was a vegetarian, an atheist and a fiction and non-fiction author. In his day his books were admired and well-reviewed – the *New York Times* hailed him as 'a prophet of Boom ... He maintains that we are at the beginning of an age of limitless abundance ... an age of immortality' – and he was employed as a futurist consultant by industry, the US government, NASA and Hollywood.[9] Fellow thinkers about the future welcomed his work enthusiastically; Alvin

Toffler, author of the huge bestseller *Future Shock,* said that FM-2030 was 'The exhilarating voice of a new, nonmystical consciousness … FM dares us to step outside our encaged historical selves, and leap to a new stage of evolution'.

Esfandiary's change of name to 'FM-2030', legally formalised in 1988, was prompted by his aim of living to the age of one hundred years, which he would have reached in the year 2030. Alas, he died of pancreatic cancer at the age of sixty-nine, in July 2000. The poignant irony of this date is that (despite what is universally thought) the year 2000 is not the first year of the twenty-first century but the last year of the twentieth century – there was no Year Zero; the first year of the first millennium was Year One. FM-2030 said that he felt himself to be a twenty-first-century man which is why he wished so fervently to live into that time. As a last effort to achieve his goal, enraged by the vulnerability of the human body to disease and decay, he stipulated that his body be placed in cryonic suspension, where it remains to this day – not frozen but vitrified – in the Alcor Life Extension Foundation in Arizona.

The books by FM-2030 on transhumanism aided the spread of the idea. *Are You a Transhuman?* is one. In his definition, a transhuman is a person who employs technologies and lifestyles to defeat the fragility of the natural human body and its limitations. 'Are you a biological fundamentalist?' he asks, and proceeds:

In the 1950s the idea of synthetic replacement parts for the body was considered at once farfetched and repulsive. People believe that such interventions would "turn us into robots". Today tens of millions of people all over the world are alive because we are able to replace non-functioning body parts with effective substitutes. If we want to extend each life far into the future we have to make still more radical changes, we cannot live for hundreds of years with these fragile limited bodies. Those who want to live should be prepared to accept profound transformations in *all* areas of life.[10]

Abbreviating 'transhuman' to 'trans', he continues, 'Trans can no longer be considered specifically human because the premises of biological terrestrial life that have always defined the human no longer fully apply. Many of the breakthroughs embodied in transhumans are nothing less than the beginnings of the eventual transformation of the human species.'[11]

As an example of the transformations already current in his day, he imagines the following conversation:

'How old are you?'

'How old am I? What does that mean? My breasts are twelve years old. My right hip is nine years old. My heart valves were installed five years ago. My new face is only two years old'.

FM-2030 wryly continues with the observation:

Imagine what a monkey wrench this throws into astrological 'readings':

'What is your sign?'

'My nose is a Gemini. My penile implant is a Taurus. My electronic bladder is a Libra.'[12]

As a clincher, FM-2030 quotes both the saying, 'Age doesn't matter unless you are a cheese' and the question, 'How old would you be if you didn't know how old you are?' The points made are apt in the light of his thesis.

These writings were among the inspirations for the founder of the Extropy Institute and president between 2010 and 2020 of the Alcor Life Extension Foundation, Max More (a name change from Max O'Connor), an Oxford philosophy graduate whose subsequent doctoral studies at the University of Southern California focused on questions of death and personal identity.[13]

The Extropy Institute ('extropy' is a coined antonym for 'entropy'), founded by More and his wife Natasha Vita-More, was catalytic for discussion of transhumanism. The transhumanist (but AI-worried) Nick Bostrom credits the Institute with providing 'the first definition of transhumanism in its modern sense' and as providing a wider forum for futurism in general and transhumanism – or in the Mores' terminology, 'extropianism' – in particular. In contrast to the chilling eugenicist theories of the early twentieth century, the Mores' views premise 'open society' liberal thinking.

Bostrom himself is one of the founders of the World Transhumanist Association (WTA), set up in 1998 'to provide a general organisational basis for all transhumanist groups and interests across the political spectrum. The aim was also to develop a more mature and academically respectable form of transhumanism, freed from the "cultishness" which, at least in the eyes of some critics, had afflicted some of its earlier convocations'.[14] Together these initiatives – More's and those of Bostrom and his colleagues – shape the current debate.

Bostrom's WTA published a *Transhumanist Declaration* stating the concept's basic principles.[15] It begins, '(1) Humanity will be radically changed by technology in the future. We foresee the feasibility of redesigning the human condition, including such parameters as the inevitability of aging, limitations on human and artificial intellects, unchosen psychology, suffering, and our confinement to the planet earth. (2) Systematic research should be put into understanding these coming developments and their long-term consequences', and after noting that '(4) Transhumanists advocate the moral right for those who so wish to use technology to extend their mental and physical (including reproductive) capacities and to improve their control over their own lives. We seek personal growth beyond our current biological limitations', ends by saying that '(7) Transhumanism advocates the well-being of all sentience (whether in artificial intellects, humans, posthumans, or non-human animals) and encompasses many principles of modern humanism. Transhumanism does not support any particular party, politician or political platform.'[16]

The rapid spread of debate that followed upon these initiatives ranges over ethics and bioethics, 'biopolitics' and the environment, and of course has embraced all the possibilities offered by AI that it sees as positive. As a particular example of the direction such thinking takes, consider the view of the philosopher Julian Savulescu on 'Procreative Beneficence'.[17] Premising the fact that selection of embryos is now possible by employing the techniques of *in vitro* fertilisation and preimplantation genetic diagnosis, which means that it is possible to test for any genetic trait such as hair and eye colour, one sees that such procedures can be extended beyond merely detecting abnormalities. In particular, in light of already-present and developing capacities to detect genetic bases not just for diseases such as Alzheimer's but, even more pertinently, personality traits such as a propensity to criminality, a general argument offers itself, which Savulescu sets out thus:

> Some non-disease genes affect the likelihood of us leading the best life; we have reason to use information which is available about such genes in our reproductive decision-making; [therefore] couples should select embryos or foetuses which are most likely to have the best life, based on available genetic information, including information about non-disease genes … [they] should select the child, of the possible children they could have, who is expected to have the best life, or at least as good a life as the others, based on the relevant, available information.[18]

Savulescu adds that this principle can be defended even if it 'maintains or increases social inequality'. A critic might immediately note that an outcome of disregarding questions of inequality is that they would tend towards an outcome in which two species of humans emerge, one selectively bred for superiority (because, say, parents can afford it for their offspring in each generation), the other left behind, serving as workers, drones or slaves (because their ancestors could not afford enhancement).[19]

Instinct finds itself in a dire struggle with logic here. The former is repelled by the idea of babies being chosen on the basis of cultural and probably also racial characteristics currently most favoured in a given society, at least by those able to access (afford) the procedures of selection. Logic – which is indifferent to sentiment, disdainful of timidity, unpersuaded by temporal and social parochialisms, and eager to get rid of bad teeth and cancer while promoting intelligence and creativity – says: 'Look, it can be done; better lives will eventuate for those upon whom it is done; therefore let it be done. To leave to the haphazard of the genetic lottery the levels of now-avoidable limitation and even suffering currently prevalent defies not only logic but a higher ethical standard than the one to which appeal is made in relation to consequent inequalities – which anyway exist as a result of the current genetic haphazard. Eventually, in an ideal setting where *all* are genetically selected for their best possibilities, inequality will diminish and perhaps vanish.'

Thus the logical argument. But there is reason for thinking that it is anyway fruitless to engage in a struggle between instinct and logic, which is that Grayling's Law applies: 'Anything that *can* be done *will* be done if it brings advantage to whoever can get it done'. The obverse of this Law is: 'Anything that *can* be done will *not* be done if it brings disadvantage to anyone who can stop it'.[20] An illustration of this latter is that if efforts to reduce fossil fuel emissions bring a cost to an economy whose associated government does not wish it to bear, that government will stand in the way of climate change targets. (The Trump administration in both its avatars acted thus.) Accordingly, as genetic modification of embryos is now possible, it *will* therefore happen for reasons beyond avoidance of heritable disease, because there will be people who will pay for it to happen. Indeed it has already happened, as witness the case of He Jiankui, the geneticist who edited and implanted three embryos in two women, all three babies subsequently and healthily born. He Jiankui said he did it to make the babies resistant to HIV.[21] He went to prison for three years. In Savulescu's world he would be rewarded.

Which way would you vote on this matter – imprison or praise? Perhaps the question is, in light of the Law just quoted, 'merely academic' as people say, for the technologies are already here or arriving, and transhumans are already among us – all those with replaced hips and knees, cardiac pace-makers, dental crowns, prosthetic limbs with AI controls, hormone replacement therapy, even brain implants to control epilepsy and Parkinson's disease. In

44

August 2025 the inner speech of paralysed patients was decoded by way of brain implants. Two months later a techno-eye restored vision to blind patients. Few if any of the beneficiaries of these neurotech advances would rather not have them.

Nevertheless it remains that the idea of drawing a line between what is acceptable and unacceptable in the way of technological supplementation or modification of human beings is fraught with difficulties. On the cards is brain-chip implantation to control traumatic memories; if that can be done, then memories inconvenient to a dictator can be controlled likewise, for example in the brain of a former close adviser who saw dreadful things being done and had developed a conscience about them. How far do we wish to go? Is there a proposal about line-drawing that could achieve consensus?

The eugenicist horrors of the first half of the twentieth century in the US and even more drastically in Nazi Germany prompted adoption of the Nuremberg Code in 1947 and the Declaration of Helsinki in 1964 as barriers against a reprise of those ugly occurrences. They relate to medical experiments and insist on consent by patients and experimental subjects. Since then the rapid development of genetics, biotechnology and medical science facilitating many more and further-reaching interventions in human health and disease have brought a new raft of ethical questions to the fore. Familiar are questions about termination of pregnancy, 'advance directives' on resuscitation, patient consent, relationships between practitioners and patients, treatment of comatose or otherwise incompetent patients, fertility treatment, and how to apportion scarce resources like MRI scanners and kidney dialysis machines, to name only the most salient. To them the question of what is acceptable in embryo editing and human technological modification adds greater difficulties.

Despite the storm of ethical questions, the positives of transhumanism can be presented as very appealing. They are well summarised by futurist James Hughes, sociology professor at the University of Massachusetts and director of the Institute for Ethics and Emerging Technologies. He writes:

> We are reaching the limits of extending healthy longevity through purely behavioral and public health interventions … To push average life expectancy beyond 90 years will require technological modification of the body. Vaccination, for instance, is the technological upgrading of our immune system's intelligence. While most people admitted to hospitals in 1900 did not survive, many life-saving and misery-reducing surgeries today are safe and routine … it is likely that by the end of this century we will be able to ensure healthy longevity for most people well past one hundred years, at a higher level of health and well-being than we can currently imagine, if we survive, and if we take the steps to make these innovations widely available.[22]

This progress will specifically involve, he says, brain–computer interfaces. At first these will be devoted to treating 'severe neurological disorders and brain injuries', but then 'access will gradually liberalize. These devices will be able to supplement memory, enable brain-to-brain and brain-to-computer communication and augmented reality, and control mood and sensation.'[23]

For Hughes the question is the *politics* of applying technology to life-enhancement, not the practicalities; these are available or on the way. He sees the most heated debates within the transhumanist movement as taking place between 'anarcho-capitalists' with their libertarian, individualistic philosophy and 'technoprogressives' who 'argue for social democratic regulation and universal provision of enhancement.'[24] Accordingly, human enhancement ambitions can be pursued by either side of the political divide, if for different reasons. But there is a complication: what do Left and Right respectively think about transgenderism and heteronormativity, given that the former are more likely than the latter to be sympathetic to diversity? Hughes notes that one reason for the rise of authoritarian politics in the twenty-first century is 'wokism'.[25] 'Increasing access to fertility assistance and prenatal selection could fit a reactionary patriarchal agenda, or might also be opposed as part of a general reassertion of a "natural" reproductive order. While the liberal regimes will impose regulatory control of enhancement technologies for safety and efficacy, they will generally leave decision-making in the hands of individuals.'[26] Seeing the connection between transhumanist aspirations and the 'techno-optimism' of the Enlightenment ideas that gave rise to them suggests that the political values associated with the Enlightenment are a natural correlate of the movement's own ideology.[27]

That would be encouraging if so. But heartening as it is to have the Nuremberg and Helsinki documents to quote, a disheartening counter is that Codes and Declarations, and even laws, are frail defences against greed and authoritarian political attitudes on race, disability and other targets of those to whom the sentiments of early eugenicists and Nazis still appeal. They are also frail defences against the loving concern of parents wishing to do everything of the best for their offspring, and keen to devote their resources to it; if their own country outlaws it, there will always be places where they can go to get it done – even illegal, secret places.

Worse, Codes and Declarations are nugatory defences against the sheer power of money. Billionaire tech titans like Sam Altman of OpenAI and founder of Merge Labs, and Elon Musk in whose business empire Neuralink is prominent and with which Merge Labs was set up to compete, include among their interests the desire either to merge with AI or to upload their brains to computers. Apple has produced electroencephalogram headphones and Meta a wristband to collect neural data; like the research done by Neuralink and Merge Labs there is much of medical value to be gained from these technologies, but it appears from what the titans themselves say that this aim is subordinate to what they really seek. Musk has spoken of people uploading memories to computers and downloading them into a new body or a robot.[28] Altman has written about merging humans with machines, either through genetic engineering or via electrodes inserted into the brain; 'we are already in the phase of co-evolution' with technology, he wrote; 'although the merge has already begun, it's going to get a lot weirder ... [and] it's probably going to happen a lot sooner than people think.'[29] Those words were written in a blog post by Altman in 2018. Matters have moved faster and further since then. If nothing else it shows how far behind the new-technologies leaders most of the world is – how far behind the curve, developments occurring before we have time to think about how to manage them, or even whether we want them.

Critics of what Neuralink and the other neurotech companies are striving for in these no-longer-science-fiction ways say that they are distracting from the really valuable aspects of research, viz. their medical applications. A *Guardian* report quotes a neuroethics professor at the Technical University of Munich, Marcello Ienca, saying that Musk's and Altman's aims are 'distorting the debate a lot', while in more robust mode Michael Hendricks, a neurobiology professor at McGill University in Canada, criticises 'Rich people who are fascinated with these dumb transhumanist ideas ... Neuralink is doing legitimate technology development for neuroscience, and then Elon Musk comes along and starts talking about telepathy and stuff.'[30] One reason for the criticism is that regulatory authorities, made anxious by more *outré* aspirations, might impose restrictions that will hamper genuine medical advances.

To transhumanist thinkers such criticisms verge on Luddism. Resisting what could be positive possibilities for humanity on grounds of small-c conservative timidities and reservations seems wrong. They argue that there are principles that can be adopted and applied, whose operation might at least limit inappropriate directions being followed; the WTA declaration states them. The question is one of balancing predictable benefits and potential harms in the light of what we value and wish to preserve in human life and experience – the kind of considerations to be discussed in Part II.

The bottom line of transhumanist aspirations is that they quite literally aim to produce *trans*humans, beings no longer human as such. This aim is utopian, and as John Carey writes in his Introduction to *The Faber Book of Utopias*, 'The aim of all utopias, to a greater or lesser extent, is to eliminate real people. Even if it is not a conscious aim, it is an inevitable result of their good intentions. In a utopia real people cannot exist, for the very obvious reason that real people are what constitute the world that we know, and it is that world that every utopia is designed to replace.'[31] Carey then observes:

> However (and this is the point over which opinion divides) to aim to eliminate real people may not be as bad as it sounds – may not, indeed, be bad at all. When we consider the atrocities that real people have committed in our own century alone, it must occur to us that there are some human types – tyrants, torturers, terrorists – that could, with advantage disappear.[32]

As ever, the challenge is to find ways of promoting upsides while eliminating or minimising downsides. Given that technical intervention in and modification of human beings is already here and widespread, and that it is increasing and going to increase further, the question is not *if* the objectives of transhumanism will be achieved – again: they already are – but *how* its further objectives are best managed. For that, we need to know what we ('we', humanity) do and do not want for ourselves – hence the discussion in Part II.

3

SPACE

The breathlessly short period of forty-two years separates the first non-stop solo transatlantic airplane flight and the first human footprint on the moon – Charles Lindbergh in 1927 and Neil Armstrong in 1969. The speed of technological development has vastly increased since then. That is why anyone looking at the state of space flight today who might be sceptical that colonisation of the moon and Mars will happen this century is probably wrong. It might appear that because moon-landing attempts are still precarious, failing often enough for it to seem that humankind is popping pea-shooters at its nearest neighbour in the sky, it would be a mistake to underestimate the prospects. Writing today at the end of the first quarter of the twenty-first century, is it reasonable to think that by the century's mid-point there will be human-crewed bases on the moon, and regular commercial intercourse between there and Earth? Readers of these words in 2050, if there are any, might have a variety of reasons to chuckle either at the naiveté or the chutzpah involved. But to extend my neck far enough to get what it supports chopped off, and defying futurists' aversion to precise predictions, I'd say the probability of it is close to a certainty.[1]

One reason for thinking so is that there are resources on the moon whose exploitation promises enormous profits to those who have, over the last several decades, already invested hundreds of billions of dollars in an effort to access them in full expectation of rich returns. Chief among these are water-ice, convertible to rocket fuel, and helium-3 gas extractable from the regolith (the dust and rubble) on the moon's surface; this gas is in short supply on Earth and a potential resource for nuclear fusion when it becomes possible – that is, when engineering difficulties are overcome; these are non-trivial – providing practically limitless, clean, safe energy for the peoples of Earth.

The major players are India, China (with Russia, a recent returner to space activity, in tow), and the Artemis consortium led by NASA. The Artemis programme was officially launched in 2017, taking over from earlier projects with much the same objectives: to return humans to the moon, there to establish a permanent base and thereafter to launch human-crewed missions to Mars. A key element is the Lunar Gateway space station, planned to orbit the moon as a base for operations on its surface. China also has advanced plans for a lunar orbital station. Artemis is a melange of public and private bodies from Japan, Sweden, France, Germany, the UK, the UAE, Australia, Austria, Canada, Luxembourg and dozens of other countries as well as the US, with the US's space agency, NASA, in the lead.

In 2020 the Artemis states participating either publicly or through private companies signed the Artemis Accords, a non-binding set of multilateral agreements establishing a co-operation framework predicated on the UN's 1967 Outer Space Treaty. The Accords' chief purpose is to govern mining on the moon, though applying to space activity more generally beyond the closer-to-Earth satellite zone already subject to a variety of agreements. The Accords' stated aim is to avoid conflicts and misunderstandings which the current near-Wild West condition of space could be all too fruitful in causing. Its provisions read well; the signatories agree to 'exclusively peaceful purposes in accordance with relevant international law', to transparency, to promote interoperability standards, to assist each other in emergencies, to register objects in space and to 'mitigate space debris', to share information and scientific data, to preserve outer space heritage, to extract space resources in conformity with the 1967 Treaty and sustainability imperatives, to accept that operations on the moon or elsewhere do 'not inherently constitute national appropriation' (that is, sovereignty claims), and to not engage in 'harmful interference with other nations' activities'.[2]

To a critic, the Accords read like an attempt to pre-empt efforts, for a principal example by the UN, to achieve an internationally binding treaty governing activity in space, one that is more robust than the now-outdated 1967 Treaty. This latter is a Cold War instrument chiefly devised to avoid the opposing NATO and Warsaw Pact blocs using the moon as a nuclear testing site or a base for military operations. Because doing the latter still occupied the realm of science fiction in the mid-1960s, it was itself a vague pre-emptive move relating to the limits of what could be imagined, at the time, about the future of humanity in space. Given that the satellite zone around Earth is now heavily militarised, and major space-active states have dedicated space military forces, the prospects for keeping military assets out of space beyond the satellite zone are dim.[3]

A critical inspection of the Artemis Accords' provisions shows that they are merely aspirational and in a number of ways weakly phrased, as is often the case with 'we'll all be good chaps' informal agreements of a non-legally-binding kind, which is what the Accords fundamentally amount to.[4] An example: saying that operations on the moon 'do not inherently constitute national appropriation' is a weasel phrase, not *banning* sovereignty claims to parts of the moon's surface or depths, or asteroids that might be rich in minerals – or eventually Mars – despite the fact that it is inevitable such claims will be made. Take the Antarctic as a direct precedent for what will happen: the Antarctic Treaty System explicitly parks pre-Treaty sovereignty issues and blocks new sovereignty claims, yet already one of the main players in that frozen region, China, is moving to assert a claim to extensive regions around its research stations being regarded as 'special interest zones' (*de facto* sovereign, by another name), presumably in preparation for the year 2048 when the ban on mining in the Antarctic expires.[5]

The drivers for an increasing space race are many and urgent. At time of writing the picture is this: leading economies have ageing populations; the geopolitical situation is unstable and fractious not least because of the weakening of the US and the rise of China, to say nothing of the many fissiparous and tumultuous local conflicts in Africa, Europe and Asia made worse, or potentially worse, by the increasing dominance of authoritarian regimes across the globe. Climate change impacts are being experienced with increasing ferocity. The world is in a volatile condition, yet the demonic drive for economic growth and profit continues, so that the coupled races for technological development and resources are hot and growing hotter. The stakes are so high that no *state* can leave to its domiciled private enterprises alone the exploitation of space as a field of opportunities for meeting some of the big economic and strategic challenges it faces. State engagement, not least in the form of public–private financing arrangements, means that if a private company in space is harassed or disadvantaged by other state agencies or companies, its own state has to get involved – here is the potential for escalation; and conflicts in space will not stay in space.

By some calculations, the GDP of the EU will be lower than that of India by the mid-twenty-first century, and in total less than 10% of global GDP.[6] Europe's ageing and shrinking population disadvantages it further. Remedies, such as immigration – needed in large numbers for economic sustainability – are politically unpopular; right-wing anti-immigration policies are a form of economic self-strangulation, exploited by populist politicians in order to gain power, but at the expense of the states' economic future. Looking to new domains of economic activity has always been a driver since globalisation started in the fifteenth century CE with maritime exploration focused on seeking resources and markets, soon followed by colonisation and the growth of empires; the same imperatives, the same human desires and practices, are present today, with space the new oceans to be sailed, explored and conquered. Countries with the resources and commitment to invest in this activity have a big advantage, a head start. But as there is more than one such head starter, it is a race, one that has been running for several decades already, and gathering ever-faster pace.

At the beginning of the space era in the 1950s and 1960s the race was run between the US and the USSR, but with different aims. The latter had the lead to begin with, being first to put satellites into orbit in the mid-'50s, and then a man into orbit at the beginning of the '60s. Galvanised by the ideological competition between the two superpowers, the US went into top gear to put human beings on the moon before the end of the '60s. It was almost wholly a 'my rocket is bigger than your rocket' stand-off, a public relations rivalry, and like the daredevils who competitively race their cars towards the edge of the cliff it was a question of who could bleed money longest in the expensive act of showing off to see who is smarter, richer, more advanced. It is reminiscent of what animal ethologists say about how alpha males in different kinds of primate societies establish dominance, either by *agonic* displays (violence towards rivals or challengers: think Putin attacking Ukraine) or *hedonic* displays (showing off, shaking bushes, dashing about making a lot of noise while thumping chests: think pop stars). Today's space race is not one whit a cosmetic affair as it was then. It is deadly earnest, and as always it is about money and power (if these are ever different).

The gold rush into space is accordingly as fraught with dangers as it is rich in positive possibilities. These latter include new technologies with a variety of advantageous uses on Earth, an extension of human imagination and creativity, a generator of new ideas at present unimaginable. Many of the developments, including achievements, made by humanity in the past involved risk, sometimes great risk. The degree of risk and the size of pay-offs correlate, which is why today's space race is so vigorous, and its continuation and growth inevitable.

The risks are not just those faced by human beings who go into space, or corporations investing mega-sums in a field where things can go expensively wrong. They include threats to Earth and its inhabitants from conflict that starts in space as a result of aggressive competition, and the risk of pathogens alien to Earth but virulent once brought here intentionally (for study, say; but it escapes) or – more likely – inadvertently.

Bear in mind that the on-Earth risk of catastrophic nuclear war is ever-present and far from negligible. And these are not the only weapons that could have the same effect; bioweapons are as bad, and in some respects even more horrific, for example by causing more lingering and painful death if done by spreading plagues or toxins, than being blown to pieces. Commenting on space and existential risk, legal scholar Chase Hamilton writes:

Space development can and does serve as a source of destabilization and conflict, both in space and on the Earth. First, as commercial interests become increasingly important and competitive, they raise the stakes of control over space and invite aggressive behaviors. In addition to the enormous commercial and strategic value of Earth's orbital planes, the asteroid belt between Mars and Jupiter is estimated to be worth quintillions of dollars ... Economic competition is historically the most significant factor precipitating global conflict, especially in conditions permitting colonial powers to exercise territorial influence from afar. These tensions are further exacerbated by the ubiquity of dual-use technologies in space ... Given this backdrop, one researcher describes space conflict as 'absolutely inevitable'.[7]

The point is reinforced by the observation that the equilibrium maintained on Earth by 'mutually-assured destruction' in the nuclear and bioweapons stand-offs is already extremely fragile, dependent on a complexity of factors that keep a precarious stability in place, but:

space-based military assets complicate these factors, sometimes unpredictably. Unlike ground-based missiles, space-based weapons have easy and quick access to attacks anywhere on the globe, leaving few opportunities for early-warning, prevention and retaliation systems to activate ... From space, it is also easier to strike without it being clear which actor is responsible, reducing the perceived risk of retaliation and therefore raising the risk of a first strike.[8]

Surveillance from space has positives; systems in the satellite orbital zone provide data about conditions that prefigure the spread of malaria in Africa, for just one of many welcome examples. But it also provides for great accuracy in pinpointing and targeting, which, on the basis of AI interpretations of activity in a hostile state – deployments of military assets, for a chief example – could trigger pre-emptive strikes also.

The satellite zone is very crowded, and space-active state militaries already have anti-satellite weapons (ASATs) of various kinds in service. Suppose one of a state's communication satellites goes offline unexpectedly; the state might infer that it is under attack and 'retaliate', thus triggering conflict. Even if none of these possibilities materialise, the mere fact of the need to be armed and ready in space poses a massive financial burden on Earth for research, development and deployment of the technologies involved, given that the imperative of winning or at least keeping up in the arms race is itself existential.

As if all this were not yet enough, Hamilton adds, 'In the context of space there is already discussion of weaponized asteroids or planetoids, mass drivers exploited for kinetic bombardment, and planet-killing nuclear, antimatter bombs, or geoengineering devices developed by enemies of the Earth.'[9] Given that science fiction has an unnerving propensity to become science fact – even, indeed, that the former is too fertile in suggestion for the latter not to be driven by it into making it fact – the unpredictability already embodied in the current state of space affairs is multiplied.

There are those who think that current trends and risks on Earth make extraterrestrial expansion a necessity if humanity is to survive. An obvious scenario is Earth's becoming uninhabitable because of climate change or devastating conflict, with humanity only surviving if it can leave Earth for places it can make habitable in space – terraformed regions of the moon and Mars, say, or an artificial planet like a giant space station.[10] Such ideas presently lie in the zone of the fanciful, but other ideas do not. Getting resources from space in a reliable, regular way might be, indeed probably will be, essential to maintaining life and its support-systems on Earth, and therefore current developments are far from fanciful; they are seriously intended. Suppose that Earth's atmosphere becomes inimical to life – a real possibility because of climate change – and that vast geodesic domes are built to house as many of the world's population as are lucky enough to be selected for survival; the energy and materials required might in significant part depend on space-based resources, their supply dependent on equipment stationed, manned and managed in space.

Other futurist scenarios see AI and robot 'synthetic life' as the inheritors of humanity when it either no longer exists or is too reduced, perhaps back to cave-man levels, by the devastations of climate, war, disease or (most likely in this scenario) all three mutually fuelling each other. This kind of view is a salve to the bleakest prognostications; it sees our best science, our legacies of Shakespeare and Beethoven, Michelangelo and Poussin, Homer and Dante, the salutary warnings embodied in our vile history of greed, war, slavery and oppression, flying endlessly out and away into space in the infinitesimal hope that it might be seen and understood somewhere by something. As a consolation, the idea that humanity's existence in the cosmos will not be tracelessly extinguished verges on the desperate.

There is a principle in philosophy known as *ab esse ad posse*, which means 'from what is to what is possible', more specifically: if something is the case, then obviously it is possible for it to be the case. Unlike some truisms, this one is important. The mere fact of the International Space Station's existence shows that lunar bases and artificial planets are possible, the challenges they pose practical and financial only. When stakes are high, such difficulties melt away. Look at what happened in the Second World War; under pressure of that gigantic worldwide struggle technology underwent developments in mere years that might otherwise have taken decades or centuries – or might never have been thought necessary. In 1939 the UK's Royal Air Force and Fleet Air Arm still had biplanes in service – Gloster Gladiators and Swordfish torpedo bombers, though only the latter saw active service. By the war's end it had the Whittle jet fighter, and the Luftwaffe had the Messerschmitt 262 jet fighter. Between 1939 and 1944 bombs were dropped from airplanes; by the latter year the V-1 unmanned flying bomb and the V-2 guided missile were falling on British cities. In 1945 two atom bombs were dropped. These enormous leaps in technology exemplify how urgency expedites advances irrespective of cost. In these cases the aim was to deliver large quanta of death and destruction on an enemy in an existential struggle. But questions about the future of humanity on Earth are no less existential, though mediated by the need – perhaps it is more accurate to say: by the *perceived* need of states and their economies for 'growth' in a situation where growth is challenged by population issues, environmental limitations, and resource costs and restrictions – to turn to space to solve problems.

In *Who Owns the Moon?* I considered the question of the risk of conflict arising from competition for space-based resources. In line with one of the chief techniques of futurist thinking, the argument invoked pertinent historical case studies: the Antarctic, the UN's efforts to get a Convention on the Law of the Sea, and one (of many that could be cited) example of the gold-rush Wild-West open-frontier phenomena in history, the late nineteenth-century Scramble for Africa by European states.[11] Their pertinence relates to the urgent need for what would in effect be a Constitution for Space, internationally applicable and binding, that governs what happens out there. Take the Artemis Accords and turn them into such an instrument, and one sees what such a thing would look like. Although words and documents are, to repeat, flimsy barriers against greed and ambition, they at least establish a guide, some benchmarks, a basis for challenge, debate and action when things go wrong.

There are some international agreements that hold up; those governing air transport are an example – arrangements regarding passage through national airspaces and air traffic management standards are paradigms in this respect. But too many others are scarcely worth the paper they are written on.

That parties to treaties will observe them only for as long as it is in their self-interest to do so is conclusively demonstrated by the Molotov–Ribbentrop Pact between Hitler's Germany and Stalin's USSR before the former invaded the latter in June 1941.

As regards what is too likely to happen in space, the Antarctic and the world's oceans outside territorial waters provide a chilling and deeply worrying augury. One might think that the disanalogies between them and space make them inutile as a basis for thinking about space, because what is at stake with them is environmental concerns – preserving the Antarctic's pristine nature, and protecting marine ecologies, neither of which applies to the moon, asteroids and Mars – but that is not the point. The point is the reluctance of states to agree to binding arrangements in the first place (as with the oceans; the US for a major example does not want to sign the UN's Convention because it does not wish any inhibitions placed on its private companies aiming to mine the deep sea bed) or to apply their principles fully (as in the Antarctic case) if it likewise restricts present or future exploitation of resources. A Constitution for Space would face severe difficulties in achieving lift-off for the same reasons; and yet these very reasons are those that presage conflict arising from competition as the latter grows more intense, fuelled by the huge investments made and appetite for the even huger returns expected. Here one anticipates the six-shooter conditions of the Wild West, the indifference to all but considerations of money and control as in the nineteenth-century colonisation of Africa.

For anyone interested in moving towards binding international governance in space, the most hopeful sign is that in spring 2025 the UN's Committee on the Peaceful Uses of Outer Space (COPUOS) produced a draft set of principles for space resource extraction.[12] It begins, as all UN documents so admirably do, 'Space resource activities shall be conducted in accordance with international law, including the Charter of the United Nations, in the interest of maintaining international peace and security and promoting international cooperation and understanding', and proceeds to recommend that space is to be free for all states to conduct space resource activities, but in such a way as not to interfere with other states' right to do the same and giving due regard to their interests in doing so, that all activity is to be peaceful (the point is stressed several times), that they are to involve no 'national appropriation' (ownership or sovereignty) claims, that the activities must not bring anything harmful back to Earth nor take anything contaminating into space, that debris on or around the moon is to be minimised, that remediation of all areas affected by extraction activities is to be carried out to the greatest extent possible, that scientific discoveries must be shared, and that space activities must be transparent – that is, publicly acknowledged. Again admirably, the recommendations include the principle that 'Space resource activities shall be conducted for the benefit and interest of all humankind and shall be the province of all humankind'.[13]

The recommendations manifest serious anxiety about the potential for conflict-engendering competition. Quite rightly so. They also manifest two weaknesses which need to be addressed before any final document emerges. The first is 'the benefit and interest of all humankind' point – again indeed admirable, but the attempt to embody this in the UN's Convention on the Law of the Sea in a practical way, by requiring that profits made from undersea mining should be shared with countries that do not have marine industries, not least landlocked ones, on the grounds that the open oceans are the 'province of all humankind' – which they are – met with a very dusty response. 'Share profits? Not me!' was the reaction; and that will be the reaction from states and private corporations seeking profits from space activities.

The second weakness is that after insisting that no 'appropriation' claims be made, the 'Possible Additional draft provisions' annex, under the heading 'Safety', and with a rash of parentheses, says:

> In conducting space resource activities, States may [after giving sufficient prior notification to all other States] establish [declare] a temporary safety [coordination] zone, or other area-based safety [coordination] measure, around a location identified for space resource activities [in circumstances] where such a measure is necessary to assure safety [, promote coordination] and avoid any harmful interference with their own [any] space resource activities.

This is the wedge that will sooner or later result in states making sovereignty claims, as is already happening in the Antarctic where, in violation of the Antarctic Treaty System's banning of sovereignty claims, China is seeking to assert its 'special interest zones'. Without an explicit rider that such zones are strictly temporary, with a sunset clause on operations which require that other actors keep their distance, the same old conflict-engendering bad habit of borders that divide Earth into states-with-armies will occur.

Note that the US, soon imitated by several other countries, passed a law (the SPACE Act of 2015) giving its nationals the right to extract, own, use and trade space resources. That is a unilateral move which immediately puts it into opposition to any UN-type effort to ensure that the benefits of space activity accrue to all humankind, which putatively has space as its collective 'province'. The crucial contradiction here is that if space is a 'commons' belonging to all humankind, how can some of humankind appropriate for its exclusive profit what thus is everyone's?[14]

In any case the semantic wrangling over the key notion of 'appropriation' is already in full swing. Examples include: does 'national appropriation' include 'private appropriation'? Is there an analogy between exploiting space resources and the freedom to fish Earth's open oceans, a question prompted by the fact that the freedom to fish is challenged by conservationists urging preservation of fish stocks – might something analogous happen with space resources?

At present the dynamic is running in the direction of a multipolar stand-off in space, with individual states and actors, or the consortia they form like Artemis or the group of states under China's umbrella (collaborating on China's proposed lunar orbital station), acting independently of other states or consortia. The UN draft proposals envision a multilateral as opposed to multipolar arrangement, but is already well behind the curve of the impetus towards the latter. The one thing that multilateralism has in its favour is that the existing default is the international legal order, which, for example, the Artemis Accords recognise in saying that its principles are conformable to 'relevant international law'. Bad actor states can and often enough do disregard such constraints – think Putin in Ukraine and Trump in Venezuela – so even this restraint is friable.

The advantages to be expected from space activity are great; the usual dilemma – how to protect the upsides from the downsides – accordingly confronts us. A Constitution for Space would help towards limiting the latter while allowing the former to flourish. The fact of the need for such a thing, together with the unlikelihood of its being achieved, tells us what the future holds in store.

A final point relates to the environmental disanalogy between the Antarctic and deep seas on the one hand, and space on the other. It is in fact not a complete disanalogy. Already mentioned is the risk that pathogens or toxins might be returned to Earth from space. One risk is that microorganisms taken from Earth into space (billions are routinely thus transported on space vehicles launched from Earth) might there mutate under space conditions and prove disastrous on returning with their hosts to Earth.[15] Although nothing living has been found in space so far, the possibility that other planets, asteroids and comets carry some is by no means ruled out; an American Museum of Natural History article about a suggestion that NASA's Johnson Space Center had discovered microscopic evidence of fossil life in a Martian meteorite (found, as it happens, in the Antarctic) explains the scepticism and controversy thus generated, but the suggestion is enough to prompt care: the existence of living organisms in bodies close enough to be accessed from Earth and returned to it cannot be ruled out completely.[16] *Caveat viator* – let the traveller beware. Compared to space wars rebounding on Earth itself, the risk of plagues from space is close to the bottom end of the probability scale, whereas conflict is at the scale's other end. So, *caveat mundus* – let the world beware.

4

THE CLIMATE

Alas, climate warnings have been issued for so long – they started in the 1890s! – that they numb us, and a desire to escape the sense of despair that rapidly settles in the face of doomsday prognostications, coupled with foot-dragging by governments, makes us avert our gaze. Together doomsday prognostications and foot-dragging shout at us that irreversible damage has already been done, and that the problems and risks continue to mount. Nearly forty years ago, at the Toronto climate conference of 1988, delegates were told that global warming would have effects similar to worldwide nuclear war. Since then emissions have continued to rise and the planet has continued to warm. The process is not linear; when trigger points are reached a cascade of adverse effects follow. Climate sceptics are unimpressed by the increasing number and intensity of severe weather events such as droughts, wildfires, floods, storms, hurricanes and abnormally hot summers. But the effects are witnessed in real time now – think of residents of cities in Arizona and California who experienced persistent temperatures over 40°C, and as high as 48°C, in August 2025. The years 2024 and 2025 have been the hottest globally since records began; extreme temperatures caused the deaths of pilgrims on their Hajj in Saudi Arabia and election workers in India. Given that dealing with these effects requires vigorous international co-operation on a war footing, something that is not happening to anything like the degree it should, makes the prospects closer to dire than dim on the spectrum of possibilities.

Not merely is it a case of 'not enough' being done, but the burning of fossil fuels is still seen as a way forward by some states and major energy companies. The Trump administration that came to power in January 2025 regards climate change as a 'hoax' and immediately set about cancelling funding for green energy projects and climate science while issuing new licences for fossil fuel extraction on land and at sea.[1] The so-called 'One Big Beautiful Bill' passed in the summer of 2025 ended most of the clean energy tax breaks designed to encourage the shift to renewables. An Executive Order signed by Trump in the first days of his return to the White House stated that it is 'in the national interest to unleash America's affordable and reliable energy and natural resource' – meaning oil and gas.[2] 'Affordable' replaces 'renewable'; 'reliable' implies that wind, sun and water are unreliable; coal, oil and gas extraction are established and there is, for the time being, plenty more of all three to be pulled from the Earth's bowels and burned into the air.

Meanwhile, South America is fast becoming one of the world leaders in fossil fuel extraction. The continent holds the world's second-largest oil and gas reserves after the Middle East. Off the mouth of the Amazon, in the Foz do Amazonas basin, where the recent discovery of a huge deepwater coral reef added to the list of the world's ecological treasures, lies a reservoir of oil potentially billions of barrels in volume, for which drilling licenses were granted in 2025. Off Guyana's coast more than half a million barrels of oil are pumped every day, making the country the world's highest per capita oil producer. A rash of oil wells covers Argentina's western plains, output predicted to exceed a million barrels a day by 2030. As these states increase oil production the continent itself is experiencing longer and more extreme storms, floods, droughts and fires than ever before.[3] A typical flash weather report from November 2025 reads:

Strong winds, a tornado, thunderstorms and hailstorms have affected the Paraná state, southern Brazil over the period from 7 to 9 November, causing several severe weather-related incidents that have resulted in casualties and damage … six fatalities, of whom five were across the Rio Bonito do Iguacu town and one more in the neighbouring Guarapuava town – both in southern Paraná state – due to a huge tornado that occurred in the afternoon of 7 November. In addition, one person is missing, 750 were injured, and approximately eighty per cent of the structures have been damaged or destroyed across the town of Rio Bonito do Iguacu, population around 14,000 people.[4]

Compared to the hurricanes that devastate the Caribbean and US states, such reports excite little attention; but local and regional climate effects are happening all over the world weekly in unprecedented ways.

If one were to aggregate the reports of huge wildfires in Australia and California, tornadoes, hurricanes, droughts, extreme summer heat, heavy rainfall and floods, occurring in the months before these words were written, all of them at levels of intensity outdoing typical recorded values, a picture of a stressed climate vividly appears. Climate change is happening: the world is warming, and at time of writing the hope that the global temperature increase can be kept at 1.5°C over pre-industrial levels has already been dashed. An *Economist* report in November 2025, headlined 'For the first time, climate models show the 1.5°C goal is dead', says the Emissions Gap Report of the UN's Environment Programme shows that the 'relentless rise in emissions since 2020 rules out even theoretical routes to the 1.5°C goal'.[5] On current projections the climate is set to warm between 2.6°C and 3.3°C by the end of the century. Only if the whole world meets the net-zero target by 2050 will the increase be kept to 2.3°C or below; that now looks unlikely. These numbers and the scenarios they imply are profoundly significant.

Although the deleterious effects of warming are likely to fall heaviest on populations in developing countries of the 'Global South', it is a mistake to think that the rich North will escape without serious problems. At the COP30 climate conference in Brazil in November 2025 Iceland expressed concerns about the possible collapse of the North Atlantic current that brings warm water up from the tropics and keeps Europe's winters mild. This current, known technically as the

Atlantic Meridional Overturning Circulation (AMOC), has collapsed before, causing the last Ice Age, which ended only twelve thousand years ago. Iceland's climate minister told the conference that his country regards the possibility of AMOC's collapse as 'a national security concern and an existential threat', and that his government is formulating strategies for worst-case scenarios.[6] Europe has to take notice; if melting ice in the Arctic disrupts the current's flow, a new Ice Age could ensue, plunging the region into extreme winter temperatures and covering it in prolonged snow and ice. Not only that, but rainfall patterns in South America, Africa and Asia would be affected, and the melting of Antarctic ice would accelerate, adding to the woes. Some scientists warn that an AMOC collapse could happen within the next couple of decades.

Mitigation rather than prevention is now the name of the game, but the continued use of fossil fuels for energy, and the relentless push for economic growth everywhere, renders even mitigation a hard ask. As regards the future, rationality requires that thinking about and planning for bad scenarios and worst-case scenarios is vital, for if mitigation proves insufficient, at least it encourages the making of preparations, as Iceland is doing. In the debate around climate change this is described by the slightly softer term 'adaptation'. Yet only eleven governments among developed countries and sixty-seven among developing countries have submitted adaptation plans to the UN's climate arm, and many of these are locally focused rather than national, two examples being the London Climate Resilience strategy and the Phoenix, Arizona,

'HeatReady' project which includes the planting of thousands of trees to provide shade and promote cooling by evapotranspiration.[7]

A contradiction in the stand taken by climate change sceptics like Donald Trump is that other aspects of their policies actually turn on an acceptance of its effects. A striking example is the Arctic's diminishing ice-sheet, opening access to natural resources and shipping in the region.[8] Trump's expansionist ambitions regarding Greenland are explained by it. The geopolitical implications extend further; Putin would like to annex Svalbard, Norway's high north archipelago, close to Russia's nuclear submarine base on the Kola Peninsula.[9]

Considering bad-to-worst-case scenarios does not divert us from trying to realise hopes that there could be a technical fix of some kind, for example a large-scale effective carbon-capture process, or an atmospheric cooling process, or some other ambitious global solution stemming from intense scientific and technological efforts to find a way.[10] Nor should it blind us to what has anyway been achieved, which might make the difference between a merely very bad scenario and a catastrophic one.

China is the example to cite here. Although it is the world's biggest producer of greenhouse gases, it is also the world's leader in renewable energy. It produces one-third of the world's electricity, generates nearly a terawatt of capacity from renewable sources, which is more than the output of 300 nuclear power stations, and earns more from exporting green technology than the US does from exports of oil and gas.[11]

Other countries are making an effort; almost 43% of the UK's energy needs were met from renewables in the year to September 2025, half of it from wind power. Over half of India's energy is now produced by renewables. The global aim set at the Paris climate conference in 2015 is to reach carbon neutrality by 2050, which if achieved would see warming held at or below 2.0°C; but most experts agree that this is not enough, because it leaves little wriggle-room given the amount of carbon already in the atmosphere and the probability that warming is a process with its own dynamic that will continue for a long time to come.[12] The carbon cycle has feedback effects, and among serious tipping-points are the release of large quantities of greenhouse gases from Amazon forest fires and methane from the thawing of Arctic permafrost. A 'tipping cascade' of multiple events triggering each other would be literally catastrophic. The Earth's geological record shows that such things have happened before, with mass extinctions resulting. But the world is warming much faster than it has ever done, because it is anthropogenic: it is caused by human activity in industry, transport and agriculture, impelled by the imperative for growth – which means: for profit.

Prognostications about climate change scenarios, known as 'Representative Concentration Pathways' (RCPs), start with the current best case, RCP 1.9, which is that warming is limited to 1.5°C and emissions decline to the point of elimination. The opposite limit is RCP 8.5, in which the world continues its present level of carbon emissions, and as a result warming exceeds 4.0°C by 2100. In this case one of the effects will be mass migrations of desperate peoples driven by flood, drought and life-threateningly hot summers from their homelands. To think of this happening only in less-developed countries of the 'Global South' is a mistake; the peninsula of Florida in the US will shrink to half its current size because of sea-level rise, and the millions living in its southern half will have to move – will become refugees. Think of that: internal refugees in the world's richest country. But of course the already-vulnerable populations of affected 'Global South' countries will experience far worse effects, one reason being that stress on resources in neighbouring countries to which hungry and thirsty people flee will be hard to cope with, because a refugee crisis of these proportions will make those of the first decades of the twenty-first century look like picnics. South Asia will be hardest hit, while the territories of some island nations will disappear entirely, for example the Maldives.

Sea level rises will permanently flood some regions, while in others a greater frequency and depth of tidal inundation will erode land and make some littoral regions uninhabitable. Sea water flowing higher up rivers and salinating them will affect agriculture in the environs. Large populations live on or close to the sea – over two billion people globally – typically on lower elevations, many vulnerable to flooding; not only they but the infrastructure of their economic activities will be affected.

In the technical debate within the climate-modelling community RCP 8.5 has met with criticism because it relies on assumptions about an increasing world population and diminishing economic growth, and also on the assumption that coal use will increase significantly. At the time that the model was devised China was opening several new coal mines every week, and the Trump administration in the US was encouraging increased resourcing of fossil fuels including coal. But although the first two assumptions hold up at time of writing, coal use is falling and renewable energy technologies are coming on-line, as described above. As a result, estimations of the likelihood that the RCP 8.5 scenario will occur vary between 5 and 35%. But as the highest-end prognostication – the worst-case one – it remains important, providing an urgent motive for seeking not to get too close to it.

Yet 'not getting too close to it' is still not enough. Bad scenarios, scenarios even less extreme than RCP 8.5, are portraits of suffering peoples, of starving, thirsty, homeless people, of people killed and injured in floods, fires, landslides and violent storms. Extreme heavy rainfall, drought and hot weather events that happened once a decade are now respectively two, two-and-a-half and four times more likely to occur today. Often forgotten is that the impact of disaster falls hardest on women in the 'Global South', whose responsibilities for children, the sick and the elderly, and for finding food and water, place burdens on them additional to other vulnerabilities. To cite just two of these latter: if drought or pollution drives girls and women further afield in search of potable water, it exposes them to greater risk of sexual assault and harassment; and if flooding is the problem, many if not most women in these societies cannot swim, and anyway traditional female clothing in such societies is likely to drown them even if they can swim. In some cases women are taking action themselves to find ways of coping with the threats; in India a women's union has set up a mini-insurance scheme to help families manage when it is too hot to work.[13] Overlooking the impact on individuals and thinking just in big-number terms is a mistake.

At the 2025 annual international climate conference, COP30, in Brazil, at Belém at the edge of the Amazon forest – the world's lung – the leaders of Japan, Indonesia, Turkey, Australia, Russia, China and most significantly the United States, were absent. Without the US, holding warming to below 2.0°C becomes a vain hope. The Paris agreement of 2015 promised that, if international efforts were fully applied and sustained, warming could be held below that level; but already warming has reached 1.6°C.

Modelling of the effects of climate change by most planners relies on the Intergovernmental Panel on Climate Change (IPCC) estimates of 1.5–2.0°C warming, less often speculating on the possibility of 3.0°C or above. Prudence in preparing for a risk of this level, given the unpredictability of how the climate will act as it warms, requires that scenario-preparation should be aimed there. It is better to be over-prepared than under-prepared. Cleaving to the numbers alone leaves out how factors other than warming itself, most significantly socio-political ones, and wider effects on the environment and all forms of life in it, interact with warming and with each other, raising the level of resulting hazard. Analysing the risk of 3.0°C or above accordingly needs to 'consider how risks spread, interact, amplify and are aggravated by human responses'.[14]

Warming has different impacts in different regions; the Sahara desert and the Siberian permafrost heating up to the same degree represent different dangers. Almost all life forms, including human societies, are adapted to ecological niches. It has been calculated that, under the pressure of climate change, wildlife is migrating at a rate of a kilometre a year further south in the Southern Hemisphere and further north in the Northern Hemisphere to cling to their adaptive niches.[15] The dependence on niches applies no less to humans, despite the technologies that make less hospitable regions accessible:

> The rise of large-scale, urbanized agrarian societies began with the shift to the stable climate of the Holocene *circa* 12,000 years ago. Since then, human population density peaked within a narrow climatic envelope with a mean annual average temperature of *circa* 13°C. Even today the most economically productive centres of human activity are concentrated in those areas.[16]

Today about 30 million people live in the very hottest inhabitable regions; with warming at 3.0°C over two billion will do so by 2070. The most predictable consequence of that is that agricultural productivity, involving significant levels of outdoor labour, will be impacted – once again, chiefly in the 'Global South', where it is already the case that scratching a living from difficult soils with repeated droughts causes much hardship. Because troubles come 'not as single spies, but in battalions' as Shakespeare has Claudius say in *Hamlet,* a climate-affected world will find it harder to deal with pandemics, wars and geopolitical instability generally, instances of these themselves the outcome of climate-induced pressures exacerbating them in feedback loops.

In a survey urging more integrated study of bad-to-worst-case scenario risks, the authors of the National Academy of Science 'Climate Endgame' paper already cited identify the 'four horsemen' of the endgame as 'famine and undernutrition, extreme weather events, conflict, and vector-borne disease', exacerbated by 'such impacts as mortality from air pollution and sea level rise'.[17] The report continues:

> The determinants of risk are not just hazards, vulnerabilities, and exposures, but also responses. A complete risk assessment needs to consider climate impacts, differential exposure, systemic vulnerabilities, responses of societies and actors, and the knock-on effects across borders and sectors, potentially resulting in systemic crises. In the worst case(s), a domino effect or spiral could continuously worsen the initial risk.[18]

These include conflicts, pandemics, political instability and economic crises. The ground for such is already over-prepared in existing fragilities in all these respects. As to disease, not only the spread of disease-carrying insects into warming areas but the appearance of novel diseases and zoonotic infections is likely, and the risk of this needs to be studied. The global economic system's high degree of interdependence is a major

81

vulnerability; as 2008 and the Covid pandemic so recently demonstrated, a collapse in any of the major markets threatens to bring all others down with it. That is not simply a matter of circulation of credit and the value of stocks and shares, but vital practicalities such as transport and food supply.

The authors of 'Climate Endgame' ask whether we could even see '"warm wars" – technologically enhanced great power conflicts over dwindling carbon budgets [and] climate impacts'. Scarcity intensifies competition; competition leads all too quickly to conflict. The survey concludes:

> There is ample evidence that climate change could become catastrophic. We could enter such 'endgames' at even modest levels of warming. Understanding extreme risks is important for robust decision-making, from preparation to consideration of emergency responses. This requires exploring not just higher temperature scenarios but also the potential for climate change impacts to contribute to systemic risk and other cascades. We suggest that it is time to seriously scrutinize the best way to expand our research horizons to cover this field ... Facing a future of accelerating climate change while blind to worst-case scenarios is naive risk management at best and fatally foolish at worst.[19]

One of the barriers to concerted global effort at dealing with climate change is the question of who bears the cost of doing so. The big polluters of the atmosphere grew rich by doing it; now developing economies are being asked to cut back or change direction to pay for the damage that the big economies have caused. It is a question of justice. This is a focus of much discussion. Among the suggestions are that developing economies in regions of the world with valuable ecologies – forests, wetlands, special habitats, coastal microsystems – should be paid by the global community to protect them. At COP30 in Brazil the host government proposed a Tropical Forest Fund to reward countries for conservation schemes. The idea is for a $125 billion bond investment whose returns would go to fighting deforestation. There is a particular aptness in Brazil's role; the Amazon is being degraded close to the point of no return, with areas ten times the size of the county of Cornwall in England being cleared every year for agriculture, most particularly ranching to supply beef. That this continues despite the immensely more sustainable alternative of protein from other sources – for example, mealworms (a delicacy in some places, but formable into burgers and steaks for less-accustomed palates) – is madness.

The Amazon forest stores nearly 200 billion tons of carbon, and exudes 20 billion tons of water into the atmosphere daily, which plays a critical role in the Earth's water and carbon cycles. With other major forests round the world the Amazon is a life-support engine; its destruction is tantamount to destruction of the world as we know it and need it to be for human survival.

Most discussion of climate change focuses on the threats to humanity. But there is the rest of the world to think about too. Human activity has harmed or even driven to extinction many species of animals and plants by degrading or usurping their habitats. In light of this, when it comes to the specific effect of climate change the estimates are more difficult to make. On the most conservative estimates about twenty species of animal have already gone *globally* extinct, with hundreds more *locally* extinct, because of climate change effects, among them snails, fish, frogs, birds and rodents, while many others – polar bears are the most publicly recognisable – are threatened.[20] Many plant species and coral reefs are equally if not more at risk; anxieties about the Great Barrier Reef in Australia are frequently aired. Again on conservative estimates, a 3.0°C warming would put as much as 30% of the world's species at *very high risk* of extinction.[21] Given the interdependence of all life on Earth, such a disruption to the planet's ecology would prove a major factor in the congeries of the interacting, mutually-exacerbating problems described by the 'Climate Endgame' authors.

Everything said to this point is inferred from the models constructed to predict how the climate will evolve and what happens as a result under different scenarios. It therefore rests on how good the models are. To be scrupulous, it is necessary to acknowledge the big challenges that climate modelling faces. The principal one is that dynamical fluid processes – air and water – are chaotic, with small local occurrences rippling out to cause major events far away: the butterfly effect (a butterfly flaps its wings in Brazil, a hurricane devastates the Philippines). Most earth system models (ESMs) rely on data derived from observational scales far greater than a butterfly flapping its wings. In an effort to take into account smaller events the models use statistical 'parameterisations'. In light of the fact that not just one butterfly but millions of them are flapping their wings, along with millions of erratic eddies and swirls in the sea, adventitious deflections of currents in the air, infrequent abrupt occurrences such as volcanoes blowing up, and a myriad other happenings, all influencing the rest and propagating yet further local effects to continue the chaotic process, the models are faced with a problem when trying to make accurate predictions, especially in regard to local and regional consequences. For example, in the case of regions of the size of Ethiopia or Bangladesh the difference of a couple of degrees in temperature can mean a greatly significant difference in the effects on vegetation, agriculture and human populations.

But understanding the difficulties of modelling the climate should not on any account be taken as a reason for climate change scepticism. As the London School of Economics climatologist David Stainforth puts it – after discussing the deficits of modelling and the need for better approaches to it – acknowledging the challenges does not give comfort to sceptics. If they are interpreted as calling 'the reality or seriousness of human-induced climate change' into question, '[t]his would be entirely the wrong conclusion. My understanding of the physics of the climate system tells me that the reality of human-induced climate change and its seriousness for our societies and cultures is beyond reasonable doubt'.[22] This gets to the key point: despite the difficulties of modelling, thinking of bad-to-worst-case scenarios is essential; it would be a dereliction to find that because we were not at an earlier time *certain* that such a scenario would rise, we did nothing to prepare *in case* it did. I am not certain that one of the tyres on my car will be punctured during a given journey, but I take a spare anyway, and ensure that it is at the right pressure.

In short and in sum, matters are thus: the world is warming, problems and risks are mounting, too little is being done, the bad-to-worst possibilities are different degrees of horrific, public attention is patchy and climate activism is rebuffed and marginalised by the short-termism of political cycles. The more that warnings are sounded the deafer too many – politicians in particular among them – become. That is the picture. We are polar bears, on slippery ice floes breaking away from the main ice-sheet and floating on diminishing fragments into very chilly waters.

5

CODA

Imponderable AI developments, the transhumanising of humanity, looming tensions in space where the bad old habits of greed and rivalry are waiting to replicate themselves, global climate changes about which the only certainty is that they are negative and potentially disastrous – these are components of an uncertain and troubling future. And they are bubbling up in circumstances that could scarcely be worse from the point of view of dealing with them adequately. There are two principal reasons for this. One is that the global political situation is fast trending in directions of political and governmental arrangements that are the diametric opposite of what the world needs, which is stable, mature governance with democratic buy-in and involvement by the world's peoples. The other is the fact that the economic growth imperative – the relentless, hungry, unremitting grasping not merely for profits but for more and ever bigger profits – is not merely unabated but increasing. The profit motive has chewed up the planet, poisoned it, exploited and oppressed tens of millions of human beings, scarcely counting this as the cost of all the progress it has also enabled. Those who oppose authoritarianism in government and destructive profit-seeking in economic activity are on the back foot, because these two factors are linked, and their coupling is powerful.

Only consider: international business is too big for any one country to constrain its activities. Yet at the same time its ability to influence governments in the states in which it operates is overweening. I discuss this in detail in *For the People*. This is an element in the increasing fragility of democratic regimes because the citizens in them feel that their governments are incapable of managing matters in ways that address the people's needs and aspirations, so they blame the system. At the same time too many in politics and big business look at the China model – an authoritarian regime running a state capitalist economy unrestrained by regulations of the kind that in 'Western' economies are intended to manage markets and protect people and the environment – and are tempted by it. The temptation might not be articulated in just those terms, but in practice the effect is the same. Trump's programme of dismantling the constitutional checks on executive power, so that what are seen as economy-hampering regulations can be chopped away, amounts to the same thing.

Between them the US under Trump and China with its steadily implemented deliberate policies have changed the geopolitical order. Trump's contribution is to destabilise and fragment treaty and trading arrangements that kept the shape of a Western alliance, rooted in the post-Second World War era, in being. As a result the parties to that alliance are making other arrangements, increasing defence spending and striking trade deals with new partners. The US hegemony over the West and for long, via it, the world, has gone. Meanwhile not just the spectacular growth of China since the 1980s but the way it has achieved it is an even greater factor. The Columbia University economic historian Adam Tooze says that China is 'the master key to understanding modernity ... [it is] the biggest laboratory of organized modernizations there has ever been or ever will be at this level.'[1] By the manner of its rise to great power status China challenges 'assumptions long embedded in Western thought – about development, political systems, and civilizational achievement itself. The familiar framing of China as "rising" or "catching up" no longer holds. China is now shaping the trajectory of development, setting the pace economically, technologically, and institutionally.'[2] Granting that there is much that is impressive about China's game-changing – indeed history-changing – rise (or as it sees matters from its own perspective, *recovery* of its position as the world's 'Central Kingdom', *Zhong Guo* from which the Anglicisation 'China' derives), it remains that its socio-political structure is inimical to the West's Enlightenment values of civil liberties and the rule of law that protects them. Enchanted by the facilitations that authoritarianism brings to government, too many – Trump, Orbán, Modi, Erdoğan, Milei – are yielding to its temptation. But if the price of China's miracle rise is the oppression of an entire people, even if alongside its economic and military power it is also a positive technology and green-energy power, then large questions need to be asked. Are human rights dispensable in return for money and armies? China says yes.

Thus it is that uncertainties are mounting, questionable possibilities are impending, just as the world is decreasingly able to deal with them. In fact the competence of the world to deal with them is going in reverse; a stark example is the way that an authoritarian regime can, with near impunity, choose to precipitate a crisis in its perceived self-interest, as with Putin's invasion of Ukraine and the resulting prolonged bitter war. Historical, tribal and religious antipathies keep smaller conflicts flaring up repeatedly in various parts of the world, replete with genocides – Gaza, the Sudan, Myanmar are examples at time of writing.

This litany of troubles is familiar enough to be too familiar, as if it is merely business as usual for our staggering planet. It is dismaying how quickly people accept the abnormality of these things as normal. In one unhappy sense, they are indeed normal; almost all of history everywhere has been no different; those of us who have lived through the last seventy-five years in the West have had an unusual experience, in historical terms, of a high level of relative peace and prosperity. The fabric of that order has frayed, and one major reason for it – ironically, and alas – is the very progress in technology that those seventy-five years capitalised on. Advances in medicine prolong life and add to the ageing burden on the 'developed' world, while half of the global population is under the age of thirty, many living in countries where their prospects are limited. Computer science has multiplied its own applications in so many ways that not a few of them have turned toxic: the viral growth on social media of misinformation, falsehood, hatred, the platforming of racism and sexism, White Supremacism, 'masculism' and neo-Nazism, is a major example.

Most past generations have had dismal sentiments about their own time. It is a common human propensity to think that the past was rosier. A psychological reason for this, applying at the individual level, is that generally speaking childhood is a better time than adulthood; a child is looked after and provided for, without taxing responsibilities, occupying a small and predictable world, in which – because a month is as a year in proportion to a child's age – summers are long and most things happen slowly. Then the exigencies of adulthood supervene, and life is not as comfortable; demands, working life, taxes, managing relationships under one's own largely inexpert direction, consciousness of limits, the fact even of death, increasingly press. This explains the tradition of pessimism that runs like a thread through the history of human thought, and highlights those periods when optimism was at a premium, as in the eighteenth-century Enlightenment.

In bleak mood one could have a field day reading such books as Emil Cioran's *On the Heights of Despair* and David Benatar's *Better Never to Have Been*. They belong to the tradition of the Bible's Ecclesiastes lamentation that 'vanity, vanity, all is vanity', and the third-century BCE Cyrenaic philosopher Hegesias' extolling of the benefits of suicide. Influenced by Buddhism's characterisation of existence as suffering, the German philosopher Arthur Schopenhauer identified the insatiable but unsatisfiable cravings of the will as the source of therefore unavoidable suffering, from which the only temporary relief is music. One could cite Kafka's *The Trial* and *The Castle* as depictions of the literal 'amazement' – lost in a maze – of the human condition, no way out possible and no explanation given. And there are plenty of dystopian writings and predictions to deepen one's sense that, perhaps, Hegesias is right.

Yet in the pixelations of human experience, in moments as short as a minute or as long as a day, people meet with good things, experience happiness, are moved by kindnesses, feel affection, enjoy something – a drink, a film, a chat with a friend. It is a trope with me to ask my students why it is that the news media are full of reports of disaster, strife and ugly things, the answer being that it is because these things are *news*; there are no headlines about shopkeepers being helpful to customers, or people making room for each other as they pass in opposite directions on the street, because such events repeat millions of times every minute around the planet. Most ordinary experience is – well, ordinary, in whatever counts as ordinary in different settings, but at least meaning not immediately threatened by bombs or starvation. And in the times when people can pause and think, there is consciousness of what would protect the ordinary good of human experience, and what would make it better. These are the things that need to be preserved and promoted as humankind steps into the complicated and anxious future in which, in the memorable phrase of my friend Adam Zeman – the professor of neurology who identified and described 'aphantasia' in which subjects of the condition cannot form mental pictures – there seems only to be 'night at the end of the tunnel'; as if we are aphantasic about the future, or at best only capable of envisioning the worst images.[3]

This is where the thoughts of Part II become relevant.

PART II

TOMORROW AND YESTERDAY

6

LETTING GO

There are plenty of things about people and society we can do without. We can do without violence and injustice, for a start, because these two evils are what do the greatest harm to people collectively and many people individually. They embrace all the other evils that befall us from outside ourselves. Violence comprehends war and murder, assault including rape, and cruel treatment. Injustice comprehends oppression, exploitation, discrimination and systemic social and economic structures that distribute social and economic goods unfairly and imprison people within limited possibilities. One could draw a tree diagram in which these headings branch out into all the ways that humans treat humans ill, mainly intentionally though sometimes unintentionally.

These are moral evils, to be distinguished from natural evils such as earthquakes, tsunamis, volcanic eruptions and plagues, plus the nature-caused but injustice-inducing unequal distribution of intelligence, talent and beauty among humans (and other animals). For the most part there is not much to be done about earthquakes and the rest; the awesome powers of nature are indifferent to the puny human and other animals that get in the way. But people are not without responsibility for the suffering they endure at nature's hands; two-and-a-half million people live on the San Andreas Fault in California, almost all of them voluntarily, and they experience hundreds of tremors every year. The residents of Pompeii were not unaware of Vesuvius's history. The two billion people who live close to the sea around the world know what a tsunami is.

When it comes to disease, the contribution people make to their own ill-health is often perfectly conscious – drinking, smoking, popping or injecting drugs, taking risks, over-eating, slopping in front of the television for hours each day. Indeed the mere fact of aggregating in cities is a health risk, because people crowd together, breathe over each other, hold onto the support pole in the subway just touched by someone who picked his nose or did not wash his hands after using the toilet. One could imagine having spectacles that illuminate the pathogens that float on people's exhalations and smear over surfaces. In our intimacies we exchange fluids with our dates and partners and breathe right into their mouths. My Great Aunt Blanche was wont to say to me, 'Stay away from people, they're full of germs', and she was right, though I did not obey. Which is fortunate, for quite a lot of this social pathogen-exchanging is good for us, strengthening our immune systems – a form of mutual vaccination. It has been sagely pointed out that too-clean houses and preventing children from getting dirty – including eating dirt – weaken us.

Still, disease and injury are ills. Suffering whether self-inflicted or adventitiously caused is not what most people want. And those who do want it cannot really be said to be suffering if suffering is their pleasure. The point about human-perpetrated violence and human-imposed injustice is that they are causes of huge amounts of *unnecessary* suffering, *avoidable* suffering, and their commonest prompts are ugly features of human nature: greed and lust, animosity and jealousy, power-hunger, ideologies that degrade some Other group to a level not worthy of moral concern so that they can be exploited or even exterminated.

Let us consider more closely some of the things we can well do without.

War, defined as conflict 'above the military horizon' and therefore meaning organised and planned large-scale conflict as opposed to a spontaneous pub brawl or gang-on-gang knife-fighting in the backstreets, is as old as recorded history.[1] The *Stele of the Vultures* dating from *c.*2500 BCE records a battle between the Sumerian cities of Umma and Lagash in Mesopotamia, won by Lagash, whose ruler Eannatum erected the stele in celebration. The stele depicts disciplined ranks of uniformly equipped soldiers accompanied by solid-wheeled carts carrying supplies and dignitaries. Eannatum is shown leading his troops into the fight, and we learn that he was wounded by an arrow but survived. With some relish we are told that vultures feasted on the enemy's corpses, hence the stele's name.

This monument is rich in information. It shows that Sumerian cities in the third millennium BCE had advanced organisational capacities for funding, equipping and training armies, which bespeaks a political structure, a centralised bureaucracy and a tax system. Equipping an army requires large-scale manufacture of weapons and armour. Fielding an army requires logistics – transport, food supply, camp facilities, in short a great deal of materiel and an additional back-up army behind the fighting troops themselves. Plans have to be laid, terrain mapped, strategy and tactics worked out. Presumably in the period before actual fighting began there were diplomatic exchanges between the cities which in this case broke down, but which in other cases – because of a desire to avoid expense and loss of life, and the general disruption – prevented fighting. If a battle needs a monument it is significant enough, and unusual enough, to warrant it. Behind every battle is a complicated story.

There are many questions to be asked about why wars happen and when war began as a persistent phenomenon in civilisation. Those who blame male propensities for aggression fail to note that even trained soldiers are deeply disturbed by it; in conscript armies, so it is estimated on good evidence, only about 20% of the troops are effective – that is, actually fire at the enemy.[2] As to the origins of war *as such*, in the sense of conflict above the military horizon, there is much debate. For example, anthropologists note an interesting fact about present-day Stone-Age societies. When inter-tribal conflicts occur, although sometimes indeed very violent, they often tend to be formulaic merely. The fighting-age men of both sides gather at an appointed spot and maintain a considerable distance from each other, whereupon imprecations and insults are hurled and a lot of dancing about and gesticulating occurs. If stones or spears are thrown and someone is injured, the encounter ends and the combatants return to their respective homes.[3] One explanation for the relatively bloodless nature of such stand-offs is that injury or death in a small Stone-Age community is extremely costly to it. When conflicts arise over existential matters – water, food, animals, women – things can get a lot uglier. But even at this level it is not *war* as such, because the communities are not organised in the way of war; they do not manufacture specialised war-only weapons, and they do not train specifically for it (not needing to, since hunting skills provide much of what is necessary in the way of stabbing, slashing, avoiding a wild boar's aggressive rush or creeping up on a selected target).

On some views war began as a result of the development of settled agriculture, thought to have become established and increasingly widespread after about 12,000 years ago, the commencement of the Neolithic Age. This was because, so the theory says, of the vulnerability of such communities to attack by nomads. A speculation arises about the reason for the world's most ancient known city, Jericho, having walls 3.6 metres high; on the face of it they exist for defensive purposes, though whether against organised enemies or floods (to which Jericho might have been exposed in 7000 BCE, from when it dates) is unknown. If the former, then the walls bespeak frequency of danger and the planning, forethought and collective endeavour required to erect such a large, solidly built structure.[4]

The battle between Umma and Lagash might have been over control of resources disputed between the cities, but a new and more ambitious dimension enters with the appearance, around 2300 BCE, of Sargon the Great of Akkad, who was not content to rule only his home territory but set about conquering an empire. He succeeded, taking all the lands between the Persian Gulf and the Mediterranean Sea, his borders extending as far east as Elam. The empire lasted two centuries, not overthrown by enemies but by climate change and the attrition of conflict between farmers and pastoralists, the latter encroaching on the former's lands in search of grazing for their herds. The Akkadians built a 100-kilometre-long wall between the Tigris and Euphrates to keep them out – unsuccessfully, as with all walls since, from China's Great Wall (in fact a multiplicity of walls) and the US fence on the Mexican border.

Likewise the Egyptians in their Middle Kingdom period (2040–1782 BCE) had armies that invaded Nubia to their south, establishing a border guarded by a chain of fortresses. In the eighteenth century BCE Hammurabi of Babylon achieved by conquest nearly as much as Sargon had, by which time the prevalence of war had long since encouraged the development of weapon technologies specific to their tasks, among them the composite bow and the chariot.

These later two military developments are significant. The composite bow is more powerful and accurate than the 'self bow' made from a single piece of sapling wood. The chariot, a swift light vehicle running on spoked wheels, pulled by trained horses expertly handled and allowing an archer accompanying the driver to fire from it, or a warrior to leap off, fight, and leap back on to get speedily out of harm's way (which seems to be the use made of chariots in Homer's *Iliad*), replaced the cumbersome donkey-drawn carts that lumbered to the war zone with their cargoes of chieftains. Both advances required preceding advances in metalwork, woodwork and leatherwork, the chemistry of glues, and the training of horses – all superior skills. Compare the donkey-drawn four-wheeled cart that carried the King of Ur in the third millennium BCE, as depicted on the Standard of Ur, trundling along at two miles an hour, with a war-chariot hurtling into the fray at ten times that speed.[5]

In *War: An Enquiry* I trace the progress (if it can be dignified with that name) in weapons technology and military theory from then until now, 'now' the age of nuclear and biological weapons, missiles, drones, autonomous AI-run systems, anti-satellite devices including laser artillery, and more. Superiority in these fields is the key determinant in the winning of wars, and the amount of treasure it consumes continues to rise and rise to this day. It is one of the most dismal spectacles imaginable, for it is about killing people and blowing things up as a way of resolving problems actual or imagined. As one of the things we could happily jettison as we move into the future, this tops the list.

Injustice as a perennial feature of human society comes close. There are two kinds of injustice most in need of jettisoning. One is economic injustice; the other is the kind that arises from the otherwise generally welcome existence of legal frameworks because of the intrinsic and extrinsic

103

problems that beset them – the latter in particular being easily remediable were we prepared to bear the money cost.

The fact of economic injustice and its toxic effects stare us in the face daily. The point needing endless iteration is that a system which channels money in ever-larger amounts into ever-fewer hands, while billions live in poverty, is unacceptable. The problem is not that some have more than others; it is the sheer size of the gap between the overwhelming riches of a few and the struggles of many, the fact that it is deliberately created, skewing the system in the former's favour – and the fact that it causes destructive social and political problems.

Income differentials are not in themselves the issue. In fact, they are justified; they are justified by the fact that some *deserve* bigger rewards than others. Such people have valuable skills, they trained longer, worked harder, are smarter or more talented, provide services others need, produce things that benefit others and/or that others want. If reward matched contribution, teachers and medical personnel and researchers would be among the most highly paid people on the planet. Almost no one grudges top professional athletes their earnings, because we admire their talent and the efforts they make to hone it. We enjoy their performances and know that they are time-limited in what they can do. If people like a pop star's songs they will buy access to her music, and she will duly benefit. Indeed, no one could object to anyone being rich, even very rich, *providing that no one is sleeping on the streets*. But people are sleeping on the streets *because* the system skews matters so that some – a very few in percentage terms – can be rich irrespective of what happens to others.

This is easy to prove. If a society wished to house everyone and ensure that they have a decent minimum quality of life, the level of community contribution to achieving this outcome would require tax arrangements that enable it. But people do not in general like to pay taxes, at least at levels that bite too far into what they want to keep for themselves. Those among the people who have lots of money tend to have proportionally lots of influence over the levels at which taxation is set (via party political donations and access to government), and in any case have resources for avoiding tax altogether – in particular by sequestering their gains in tax havens, which deprive national incomes of billions. Paying accountants and lawyers, and donating to political parties, are a small cost of business with big returns for such people. They keep the system skewed, aided by politicians' reluctance to risk not being re-elected by asking the community to pay more for greater overall social decency. So the poorest pay with how they live their lives, and even with their lives, so that others can live in luxurious homes and cruise on private yachts.

The social injustice of this arrangement is exacerbated by the fact that society as a whole provides the conditions in which the rich can get rich. It provides education for the workforce, policing of social order, a legal system that protects patents and enforces contracts, gives bail-outs to troubled banks – in short: it constructs and pays for the setting in which business can safely be done. The successful businessman profits from this community investment, and then works to ensure he does not himself have to pay too much into it.

In 2025 the richest 1% of the world's population owned 21% of its wealth. The next richest, constituting 9% of the world's population, owned 37.3%. Thus nearly 60% of the world's wealth is in the hands of 10% of its population. The rest is unevenly shared among the remaining 90%.[6] The assets of the very richest individuals are measured in multiple billions of dollars, which is a staggering consideration; in order to grasp its meaning one needs a visualisation, like this: a million seconds on the clock is nearly two weeks, a billion seconds on the clock is *thirty-two years.* Not long before this writing Elon Musk was awarded a $1 *trillion* pay package by Tesla.[7] A trillion seconds is *31,688 years.* One has to ask what an individual can do with this kind of wealth. Though not literally unlimited, as a resource from which to make impactful contributions to medical research, the arts, education, social justice initiatives, helping people out of poverty and encouraging talent, the prospects are sky high. Some very rich people are philanthropically minded and have done, and do, good things; Bill Gates is an example. Others use the power that such wealth confers to interfere in politics in questionable ways – Musk is a supporter of the far-right Reform Party in the UK, having helped Trump to victory in 2024. One of the ways they interfere consists in ensuring that they keep as much of their wealth as possible.

A supplementary observation is that the weapons brandished by militias in Africa and the bombs set off by terrorists in the cities of India, Pakistan and elsewhere are not paid for by penny contributions, but come not just from governments using covert methods of destabilising rivals and

106

also from non-state organisations with access to wealth. And this is to say nothing of the arms industry, which profits to the tune of hundreds of billions of dollars annually from producing instruments to kill, maim and destroy, and for which nothing is more profitable than chronic long-lasting conflicts requiring ongoing resupply.[8]

Despite internal debates and controversies about the matter, Scandinavian countries remain the world's best exemplars of what can be done in the way of reducing inequality and promoting social decency. They have high taxes and high levels of spending on social services, health and education, seen as an investment in human capital which provides economic dividends and promotes trust and stability.[9] Other factors, such as tradition and small national populations, play their part in Scandinavia, but a wide consensus on tax and spend policies is key. These countries are a standing admonition to a system that in so many places elsewhere causes and maintains high levels of inequality *deliberately*, and which are therefore unjust and damaging.

A second thing we wish to leave behind is not only social and economic injustice but the injustices in the institutions of justice themselves. It might seem curmudgeonly to see law as a site of injustices given that 'the rule of law' is a precious principle. And so it is, at its best; long ago Livy wrote at the beginning of Book II of his history of Rome, *From the Founding of the City*, that the glory of the Roman Republic lay in its having ejected the haughty Tarquin kings and put 'rule of law' in place of 'rule by men' – rule by capricious, tyrannical men, as men with too much power have a tendency to become, as we remind ourselves with Lord Acton's dictum that 'power corrupts, and absolute power corrupts absolutely'. Julius Caesar's threat to restore 'rule by a man' led to his murder. Alas, the Republic fell anyway, to usher in the epoch of the Roman Empire, some of whose rulers were full-blown tyrants.

'Rule of law' is not, note, 'rule *by* law' in the sense of palpably unjust laws, such as Hitler's 'Nuremberg Laws' against the Jews, passed on purpose to enact discrimination and oppression, their aim (at that point, before the gas chambers) being to drive Jews out of Germany by making life in it untenable for them. Rather, 'the rule *of* law' denotes embodiment of the principles of equality before the law, protection by it, and access to its remedies, governed by rules of due process and transparency, and conducted by an independent judiciary.

Yet even this ideal is infected with problems. For one thing, laws are made by people, and reflect attitudes, principally moral attitudes, from which flow choices about what to count as crimes. Laws make criminals; whereas some things are obvious candidates for criminalisation, such as murder, rape, cheating and stealing, others are far from obvious, such as homosexual sexual practices, drinking alcohol, expressing contempt for religious beliefs, and exposing areas of the human body traditionally covered up. Laws of this kind might slip into the 'rule *by* law' category in that they apply discriminatory attitudes, expressing the distaste some have for gays, alcohol and nudity. There is a difference not of degree but of kind in refusing to tolerate murder and refusing to tolerate nudity. Nevertheless, in the panoply of laws in every state there will be some that are ethically questionable on these grounds, and their enforcement raises questions about their justice.

For another and more general thing, laws are admittedly blunt instruments, in that they are promulgated to cover *classes* of cases among which *individual* nuances of circumstance might create difficulties about how or even whether they should be applied. It often enough happens that the correct application of a law will not accord 'natural justice' to a party in a particular case. For those denied natural justice by official justice, the outcome is bitter, and rankles. But it is a condition of membership of society, in the interests of the general well-functioning of its institutions, that such outcomes be regarded as a cost of the other and usually greater benefits that a system of justice provides. A system of justice has to accept some injustices to work.

A big problem concerns access to the law. Legal action is very costly, too costly for most. Expensive legal advice promises better outcomes for litigants and indicted persons; therefore those who cannot afford it are at a disadvantage in comparison. Because everyone is putatively 'equal before the law', the fact that people come unequally well-represented before its tribunals is an injustice.

In thinking about what to leave behind as we move into the future, separating law from morality and ending it as a field of private enterprise for its practitioners – thus, ejecting the profit motive from it – would be desiderata. The second of these requires major public investment, because the law is immensely complex and demands great expertise, and expertise merits reward. The level of reward is what imposes barriers to equal access to the law, *de facto* making people unequal before the law in violation of a fundamental rule-of-law principle.

The same problem therefore arises as in the decent-society case – in fact, is a dimension of it: which is that only if everyone contributes enough to the common pot through taxation can there be true justice in the law's workings.

'Justice' itself is a rich and debated concept. A distinction is required among at least four senses of the term. In its application to law it comprises procedural, restorative and retributive justice. The first relates to how the law's application is effected – principally policing, the court system, and the rules governing both. The second relates to putting right what has gone wrong and repairing relationships within society. The third is about exacting punishment for wrongdoing. The fourth sense, different from these, relates to public policy matters; this is 'distributive justice', the equitable apportionment of goods and duties.

A good definition is provided by the Legal Information Institute of Cornell University's Law School, covering both the principle of justice and its institutional expression. On the principle it says, 'Justice is the ethical, philosophical idea that people are to be treated impartially, fairly, properly, and reasonably by the law and by arbiters of the law, that laws are to ensure that no harm befalls another, and that, where harm is alleged, a remedial action is taken – both the accuser and the accused receive a morally right consequence merited by their actions.' On the institutional aspect it says, 'Justice is a legal structure or system that is designed to judge in a general sense who should be accorded a benefit or burden when the law is applied to a person's factual circumstances.'[10] If there were a nit to pick in this it is the reference to 'morally right consequence' in the definition of the principle. Apart from the disputes there can readily be about what is 'morally' right, there is a vigorous debate about whether punishment and the forms it takes are themselves morally acceptable, given that it involves harm to the person punished: loss of freedom, violation of family life, distraint of possessions, even death where executions are performed. A major factor in judicial punishment is protection of society from the harms caused by malefactors, and this is a matter of expediency, not morality. Exacting retribution as a way of satisfying victims of crime – relatives of murder victims can be present at executions in the US – is another expediency. Both have their justifications, but they involve treating the doing of one harm (to the prisoner) as less severe than another harm (done by the prisoner to his victims), licensed by the utility of doing it for protecting society and compensating victims at least psychologically. There are other though fainter hopes: deterring would-be criminals, dissuading those punished from offending again, and reforming them from their bad ways.

The chief point at issue for present purposes, however, is *social justice.* That means a fair and inclusive society, in which each member is treated with equal concern. 'Equal concern' is not the same thing as 'equal distribution', because this latter can be *inequitable,* as demonstrated by this example: an athlete in training might require 5,000 calories a day, an elderly person 1,600 calories a day, but if you oblige each to consume the median amount of 3,300 calories a day, you treat both unjustly. Fairness is not equality but equity. The great desideratum is for an equitable society, which means a society whose structures are not designed to privilege some at the expense of others, but where all have genuinely fair treatment and fair chances if they will take them.

Another obvious candidate for what we want to leave behind is disease both physical and mental. Very few would disagree with this, and those few consist chiefly of two parties, viz. those who make money out of people being sick, and those who enjoy being sick or portraying themselves as sick. (Almost by definition, these latter really are sick.) Throughout history people have striven to prevent illness occurring and curing it when it comes. The ancient physicians – Hippocrates, Galen, the Asclepiades – prescribed a combination of moderate diet and regular exercise as the best prophylactic, and they were of course right. But even these preventatives do not guarantee health because, as everyone knows, pathogens and injury, stress and the mere fact of ageing, assault humanity and overwhelm its natural defences at times: this is a given of the human condition.

Before the very recently acquired miracles of modern medicine the resources available to doctors were few and sometimes positively harmful. For example, mercury treatment for syphilis was only partially successful in treating primary infection, useless in the secondary and subsequent stages, and in itself poisonous. In pre-antibiotic days (penicillin was first used in 1941, becoming widely available after the Second World War) there were few other defences against the scourge of infectious disease. Tuberculosis has been a principal one of these probably since *Homo sapiens* appeared on the scene; it is found in Egyptian mummies, it was correctly diagnosed by Hippocrates (under the name 'phthisis') who recognised it as especially fatal for young adults, and it carried off John Keats, Emily Brontë, Frédéric Chopin, Robert Louis Stevenson and D. H. Lawrence among many others. Today one-third of the world's population carries the TB bacillus and is at risk of developing the active disease.[11] But treatment for it is now far more effective than long stays in sanatoria up mountains, drinking milk. (Ironically, unpasteurised milk was a common vector of the disease.)

Influenza is another familiar scourge. It is repeatedly pandemic; since the major crisis of 1919 in which twenty million people died worldwide, there have been less acute pandemics, in 1957–8, 1968 and 2009. I was a very sick child in the first of these, aged eight at a boarding school, the only patient left after the school was evacuated. I proposed marriage to the sweet young nurse who looked after me, which she very kindly said she would answer when I was older. (This illustrates the truth in the saying attributed to Confucius, that 'man who wants to marry nurse must be patient'.)

The first flu vaccines approved for general use became available in 1945. Each year a hurried research process gets underway to identify what strain of flu is likely so that an appropriate vaccine can be manufactured. It is generally but not infallibly successful, and always improving; the post-1919 pandemics each had mortality rates of about a million people, but according to the Mayo Clinic vaccination prevented seven million illnesses, three million doctor visits, a hundred thousand hospital stays and seven thousand deaths in the US in 2019–20.[12]

Covid is another story. It illustrates the danger of new pathogens, including zoonotic ones – ones that leap from animals to humans. Avian flu, Ebola, the Marburg and Nipah viruses, found their way into people from a variety of animal sources. Covid is one such. Close contact with animals and their excretions, and eating infected animals, is the bridge. In some cases viruses are harmless to their animal hosts but devastating to people. Viruses rapidly mutate, quickly adapting to new hosts, able to do so because they have short generation times and exist in huge numbers. A typical course for a viral disease is that it starts by killing lots of people and then, because the virus does not want to lose its host – at least, too quickly – it therefore adapts, the illness it causes becoming less severe. This appears to be the case with Covid, which is taking its place alongside flu as a recurrent endemic affliction. It took decades for flu vaccines to be recommended for everyone, at first chiefly being reserved for the vulnerable; that is the current situation with provision of Covid vaccines, a policy that will undoubtedly change as the cost of their production declines. (As usual, the money nexus operates. The people who make these decisions get the vaccine.)

Vaccine scepticism is bringing back measles and doubtless other afflictions which were on the way out as a result of universal childhood vaccination programmes. It is always wise not to underestimate human irrationality. But the desideratum for the future is that communicable disease can be eradicated, as smallpox has been; not just tuberculosis, measles, mumps, scarlet fever, and the like, but malaria and other diseases that kill, blind and cripple people in the tropics, and which – with climate warming – are creeping into regions hitherto free of them. This latter point suggests that self-interest will galvanise the wealthier parts of the world to pay more attention to eradicating these diseases, along the lines of what happened when pollution of the Thames in London, which killed thousands of cholera victims in the poor East End of the city, crept far enough westward to assault the nostrils of Members of Parliament in Westminster, who were at last (in 1858) moved by the stench to vote money for a sewage system. But to repeat: that happened only when the stench and its portent reached them.

This latter point identifies what needs to be left behind: treating health as something to be traded against cost and submitting its best prospects to the profit motive. Again, the cost of pharmaceutical research, training doctors and nurses, building and equipping hospitals, and running public health programmes is huge, and the rewards to those engaged have to be appropriate. To do it even *at* cost would be a massive call on the public purse, which means: to what individual members of society contribute through taxation. As with economic justice and legal justice, healthcare provision therefore requires a sufficient degree of willingness on the part of those who can prevent it from being done (Grayling's

Law again). When it comes to taxes, in the current state of affairs, that means almost everyone; which brings us to the next thing we could well leave behind, namely, what might be called the *civic deficit.*

In the ideal we want society to be more civil, which means people being kinder, more empathic, more prosocial, more co-operative, more altruistic. In the age of neoliberal capitalism, which can be dated from the beginning of the last third of the twentieth century, individualism has ballooned from its naturally very high level in human beings to altitudes once the preserve of historical elites only. Recall Mrs Thatcher's 'there is no such thing as society.'

A call for a more communal society acting with greater collective agency immediately suggests a range of nostrums from communism to communitarianism, thus traversing the political spectrum from far Left to centre. History has many examples of movements and groups who argued for positions on this range, together with their attempts to put them into practice. There are even versions that in other respects sit on the further right of the spectrum, such as Plato's ideal republic, but as theoretical positions go this is unusual. Generally it is when collectivist programmes are put into practice that they turn into tyrannies imposed by the collective – or more accurately: those in charge of it – over individuals, as in Stalinist Russia and 'communist' China. Christian utopians, Hussites, seventeenth-century Diggers, Owenites, the Amish, utopian socialists, Israeli kibbutzim – there are many more – are examples of collectivist endeavours. Tyranny arises when stubbornly recalcitrant human nature has to be coerced into conformity with collective norms. At a sweet spot on the spectrum sits a socially liberal, economically just and democratic ideal about two-thirds of the way from far Left to centre, where the state does not coerce individuals to serve the communal interest, thereby restricting their liberty, but where instead individuals buy in – literally – to the project of a decent society by their willing subventions. In practice, if not again in either name or theory, that is where most European and certainly Scandinavian societies positioned themselves in the second half of the twentieth century. Even in these societies, tension persists between collective aims and how much individuals are prepared to sacrifice on behalf of them. In the US, social democratic ideas have always been on the back foot, opponents of 'liberal' views hyperbolically pretending to construe 'liberal' as virtually meaning 'communist', a name of particular malediction there because it implies everything diametric to the extreme individualism of American orthodoxy.

The worst things about individualism are selfishness and indifference to the plight of others – indifference at least in practice, but that is where it counts (you see suffering on a TV report about a far-away place, feel sorry for the people there, but do nothing, not even sending a donation). People are naturally protective of their own interests and those of their close circle, especially family; it is a familiar observation that the degree of concern for others falls away proportionally with the distance from the self and inner circle. This proclivity is innate, a result of evolution. Yet at the same time and for the same evolutionary reason, humans are social animals, and have equally innate abilities to recognise what condition other people are in, emotionally and physically, and to respond or at least react to what they thus discern. Enough of the latter prosocial impulse exists to produce degrees of social cohesion sufficient to serve individual needs; we do better in society than outside it. When a society begins to have problems and needs that require greater input from individuals to the collective interest, the question of 'how much' arises. This is where the tax issue bites. In small communities, the benefit of helping others has visible returns; you join others to help in building someone a house, they join you to help build your house. You join others to help the defence of your community because you individually are thereby defended. But in large populous societies the effect of your tax contribution seems remote to the point of invisibility. You do not recognise their immediate effect though they are all around you, in the streetlights, the passing ambulance, the patrolling policeman, the paving stones under your feet. Most people do not see the inside of prisons or, very often, emergency rooms at hospitals. Yet they are paying for both, to promote the aims for which both exist. This lack of recognition, coupled with the inconvenience of paying taxes, has the effect of restricting what society collectively does for itself. And the more consumerist, advertising-inflamed and money-oriented a society gets, the more individualistic it becomes.

One effect is that interpersonal relationships degrade. At the extreme of normal life (that is, before the point of overt criminality is reached), the spectacle of anti-social behaviour of the kind associated with rowdy, swearing, spitting, littering, middle-finger-cocking youths is a marker. Picture a scene: a crowded underground train, a pregnant woman standing at the support pole and clinging precariously on, a nearby hooded youth sitting with widely spread knees, perhaps engrossing two whole seats, absorbed in his smartphone. Picture an even worse scene: a huddled figure of someone sleeping, or in drug-induced unconsciousness, in a shop doorway at night. The first scene illustrates a diminution of a sense of civil mutuality; the second illustrates society's reluctance to do enough, collectively, to provide minimally decent conditions of life for its least able members, and to provide alternatives to the palliation some of these seek from drugs or drink.

Some will say in response that the education system is letting us down, and that at least many of the poor and addicted are that way through choice, laziness or fecklessness. It is certainly true that an underfunded and stretched education system is struggling to achieve desired literacy and numeracy levels, leaving little room for inculcating even the rudiments of civic awareness. No doubt the charge against the poor holds true of some; no doubt welfare provision has its free-riders and exploiters. But the desire to deny free-riders and exploiters a share of the money one earns and sends off in taxes is like curing a headache by shooting yourself in the head. For only think: what would it be like to live in a country without communal provision of basic amenities? No sewage system, no rubbish collection, no police, no streetlights at night, no one to help if you have an accident – the Hobbesian (Thatcherian?) nightmare of the brutish situation in which there is no society, only individuals out for themselves. In places like the US and South Africa where inequality is so enormous that some actually live in conditions like this, others who can afford it live in 'gated communities' – behind defensive walls – where (again because they can afford it) they privately purchase the services that make life tolerable.

It can be left to readers to consider where, going into the future, the balance between the individual and society lies in respect of the former's contribution to the latter. I personally would say: at the sweet spot indicated, which has among other advantages that it does not fall foul of the problem Isaiah Berlin identified as besetting all small-l liberal societies, viz. the irresolvable conflict between liberty and equality. This is because the equality it emphasises is equality of concern, equality before the law, equality of opportunity, and *equity* – fairness – in all else.

There are far more radical proposals than this for what should happen in future, some of which have already been tried though their proponents will say not *properly*, not *really*, at the state level, from anarchy to communism. Versions of these at local and community levels can work, best in the form of co-ops democratically run. The trouble with anarchism, the most extreme form of libertarianism (not at all the same thing as liberalism, small-l or otherwise), is that sooner or later, and usually sooner, the strong trample the weak. Law and conceptions of rights have developed to protect the latter from the former. Historical socialist and communist regimes have been bedevilled by the slide to forms of authoritarianism required to get everyone into line for the collective purpose. That does not have to be so, but it needs a somewhat revised version of human nature to make them work, a perfecting of a kind of Scandinavian willingness to share benefits and obligations voluntarily. It is an oddity of the debate about these matters that more radical and demanding proposals about restructuring society, which involve much straining after effect, offer themselves as revolutionary, whereas advocating the sweet-spot idea – which to the activists in these various causes looks tired, worn, hackneyed and old-hat – is actually the most revolutionary of all.

Not only the activists for radical causes but people in general are apt to glaze over at the mention of a key point in the sweet-spot notion: that of human rights. But the fundamental importance of these for a just and equitable society cannot be overstated. If everyone respected everyone else's human rights unreservedly, many of the problems in the world would simply vanish.[13] Going into the future, that is a minimum necessity for the possibility of good lives in good societies, because respect for rights corrects the injustices here discussed, and numerous others besides. The more radical proposals would, on this basis, quite likely work also.

7

THE IDEA OF VALUES

A central plank of Aristotle's method was to start by canvassing opinions and beliefs about a given subject-matter that interested him. It involved observing what people said and did as revealing what they valued and the assumptions that lay behind the valuation. He mined the data for this enterprise from observable trends in public opinion as well as the theories and arguments of thinkers, these latter in important part consisting in critiques of the commonly held views. Between them, commonly held views and critical reflection on them constitute a dialectic, which as it proceeds exposes the most significant points to be considered. For example: people typically say that they wish to be happy. On being pressed as to what they mean by that, and what would make them so, much emerges, as if one were stripping away topsoil to reveal the rock formations below – the structure, the underlying geology of relevant desires, aims and attitudes.

In line with this approach, three overlapping sources of data offer themselves for thinking about values. From the life of society around one a huge word-cloud rises, leaving its deposit on many surfaces – the cinema screen, the pages of magazines and newspapers, the content of social media on smartphones, the behaviour of people shopping, the chat in bars and coffee-shops – from which an anecdotal but largely accurate picture can be formed of what a society's members value in that place and time.

That is one source. Another is philosophy, where the critique of these values is found, not just of historically parochial versions of them but the persistent themes among them, observable in human experience more widely.

A third is literature in general and the literature of utopia in particular. Novels, poems, plays are lenses onto the activity generated by what people value – which in other words is to say 'what people want' – whether authors are focusing their lenses consciously or unconsciously on that issue. In effect literature distils the word-cloud rising from society into narratives about what people want, and what they therefore do, in relation to the values motivating them.[1]

The history-long tradition of utopian literature – 'utopia' means 'nowhere' – is especially interesting, because in both forms of *eutopias* (good places, human paradises, the 'eu' prefix meaning 'good') and *dystopias* (bad places and situations), the essence of questions about what *is* and what *should be* in the way of value is their very point.

From the social word-cloud and its literary distillations a great deal appears, allowing largely safe generalisations, so safe as to be beyond obvious. We learn that people value having someone to love and be loved by, family, friends, being appreciated and standing in good regard, and – at least for many – having a purpose and achieving something. We learn that they enjoy being amused and entertained, relaxing, laughing, having time off from demands. We learn that security – at least enough money, a home, a place in society – matters immensely. We learn what makes people miserable: loss, illness, failing, rejection, exclusion, loneliness, insecurity, anxiety, being victims of injustice and discrimination; and that these cause low self-esteem, deracination and depression. These negatives are the reverse of things valued, their mirror-image. One could read off from either list what the other list will contain.

The words people use to characterise how they feel, relative to how they are doing on these respective lists, are 'happy' and 'unhappy'. That is interesting, because they show that 'happiness', which commonly denotes a positive emotional state as an occurrent sentiment, actually does not mean this but instead means a *condition of life*, in the sense of the character and circumstances of the life being lived.[2] If in general the first set of desiderata are realised, then one is happy in that sense even if one at present has toothache, a broken limb or a quarrel with one's spouse over whom to invite to dinner. That is what 'happiness' means in the US Constitution's phrase 'life, liberty and the pursuit of happiness'. Better terms for the positive *emotional* state people loosely describe as 'happiness' are gladness, joy, cheerfulness; such feelings are likely corollaries of a happy condition of life but, as the examples just given show, their absence for particular local reasons does not subvert the condition. The things that make people miserable are subversions of that condition by virtue of the degree and duration of negative sentiment, typically associated with the lack of happiness's constituent features – mutual affections, security, purpose, and the rest.

There is a disconnect, a radical one, between this anecdotal account of things socially valued and what many philosophical traditions emphasise. The ancient Greek philosophers valued *virtues*, four in particular: justice, wisdom, continence and courage.[3] Only the last of these is carried over from the concept of virtue preceding the 'axial revolution' that occurred either side of the fifth century BCE, in which *civic and moral* virtues, in a remarkable revolution of thought owing to the philosophers, replaced the *warrior* virtues exemplified by Homer's heroes, not least Achilles.[4] The warrior virtues are heroism, skill in fighting, preparedness to kill and die for one's cause whatever it is, indifference to survival provided that glory is achieved. 'Virtue' derives from 'vir' which in Sanskrit means 'warrior', 'hero' and in Latin 'man' in the sense of male human being (not 'humanity' in general). Justice, wisdom and continence (this last in the sense of self-restraint, moderation) might well be exemplified by a Homeric hero, the first two even on the battlefield, but they are not the defining characteristics of the hero. By contrast, in the new world introduced by the axial age, though prowess at arms was still valued in its appropriate setting when needed, such things as individualistic aggression and skill with sword and spear were not what was required in the civic arena, the *agora*, or in personal activity, both constituting the setting of most of life.

As an illustration of the disconnect at issue, consider that a common desire of most people in most places and ages is to be rich. 'Rich' means abundance, having a lot, being wealthy, having very much more than is sufficient for basic needs. The philosophers respond that having a sufficiency for basic needs is itself riches: 'He is rich who has enough' says one dictum. The implications go further. For the philosophers, the things truly worth having – health, peace of mind – cannot be bought, yet both are actually threatened by having riches, and even by just desiring them. Having them might lead one to health-compromising indulgences. It might make one anxious about keeping them and protecting them from thieves. It will make one a subject of jealousy and resentment. Even merely desiring them is a burden; it is a source of dissatisfaction, and motivates restless activity aimed at getting them. A common phenomenon is that acquiring riches does not appease the hunger for more; perhaps one does not hear much about people who, having become wealthy, sit back and enjoy their fortune, but one sees plenty of cases of rich people vigorously exerting themselves to get richer.

Religion introduced 'faith' and 'obedience, submission, to the gods or God' as virtues. On philosophical grounds neither is persuasive. Faith implies accepting what reason and evidence reject; a better alternative is scepticism in its positive sense of investigating the validity of the grounds for a view or claim before accepting or rejecting it. 'Submission' to what a tradition and its priests say is an act of *heteronymy*, that is, handing over control of one's life to someone or something

126

else, in contrast to *autonomy*, deciding and acting on one's own responsibility for doing both.[5]

Buddhism and Jainism – which in their original forms are philosophies not religions because neither of them premises belief in the existence of deities who legislate what form human life should take – both regard life as suffering and therefore identify the ultimate good as escape from existence, in at least the form of escape from selfhood into the Absolute. But they specify virtues to be embraced while stuck in this suffering-inducing illusory realm, viz. the world, chief among them compassion, continence, and *ahimsa*, doing no harm.

Even so summary a survey of philosophical views shows the respects in which, and the degree to which, they differ from commonly held attitudes about what matters. There are overlaps; some philosophers, Aristotle and the Epicureans being prime examples, valued friendship very highly. Epicureans, Stoics and Sceptics among the ancient schools valued *ataraxia*, peace of mind, which is what commonly held views about relaxation embody. The common aversion to suffering and misery provides Stoics, Buddhists and Jains alike with their starting point in recognising that suffering is unavoidable in life's experience and therefore training themselves to endure (Stoics) or ultimately escape it (Buddhists, Jains). To that extent one sees a coincidence in desiderata. The difference lies in the routes selected to their realisation. Most in the contemporary West endure and some meditate, but the latter is a minority avocation, and endurance chiefly proceeds by way of distraction in all forms – which include the chemical means of drink and drugs. In fact the same distractions have been employed by many in all places and ages; it would seem that *Homo sapiens'* conscious intelligence is enough of a burden enough of the time for distraction to be necessary from the thoughts and feelings, the experiences, it makes possible.

But there is a larger difference. In almost all contemporary societies consumerism is a dominant feature. At its root is the belief that to *have* is to *be*. On this principle, one manifests oneself via one's possessions, house, car, clothes, holidays, job, associates, standing, the persona they collectively constitute. One's being, and the meaning of one's life, are imported from without, chiefly by purchasing them. The philosophies are orthogonal to this principle. The things to *have* that make one what one *is* are not things one can buy. They are sourced from within, from contemplation and self-discipline. This austere, not to say rebarbative, principle is unattractive as an alternative to dining out and flying to sunny beaches for a holiday. The fact that so many dislike living the philosopher's life perforce, because they are poor and have few options for escaping poverty, is no great recommendation for it either.

What, then, is one to say about value and values?

To get some perspective, a distinction has to be drawn between *intrinsic* value and *instrumental* value. Something intrinsically valuable is valuable in itself, not as a means to or adjunct of some other and usually greater value. An instrumental value is a value of the latter kind; it is a resource for attaining a greater value.

Take as an example *education as a value.* Is it intrinsic, or instrumental? Is knowing stuff in itself a good thing independently of what knowing it enables one to do or be? Most would say that is an instrumental value – it is better to know about the world, the past, what has been said and done, what possibilities there are in human experience, how things work, how to think in an informed way, how to deal with challenges, how to apply the experience of humankind distilled in what we learn, *so that* we live better. 'Living well' in this sense – not necessarily a material sense – is the higher value served by education. For the most part education as what is provided in schools and colleges has an explicitly instrumental character in that it is preparation for getting a job and paying one's way. This banausic aim has narrowed education from the more idealistic project of helping people to have a large, informed view of things that makes them not merely economically useful to themselves and society but apt and productive all round, as citizens of the world, lovers, spouses, parents, friends, colleagues, neighbours, voters, travellers, participants in social life and contributors to it – and as people who are self-aware, better equipped as experiencers, better able to see what there is to be seen and respond accordingly. In this way they can live more richly, more alert to being alive and in the world. But this is still to think of education as an instrumental value, because it enables these other values. An indication of education's instrumentality is that it is not the only way to achieve these higher goods; when it works it is *sufficient* for their attainment, but it is not *necessary*.

The pair of concepts just employed is useful. The difference between necessary conditions and sufficient conditions can be illustrated as follows: it is sufficient for my being in Paris that I got here from England by train, plane, car, helicopter, submarine or on foot. None of these is necessary for getting from England to Paris. But it is necessary for anyone's being in Paris that he or she exists, has eaten enough food over the years since birth, and took some form of transport capable of moving a human-sized object from one location to another (except for the case in which the person in question was born in Paris and has never since left). Another example: the conditions necessary for a fire to start are oxygen, sufficient dryness of the materials involved or alternatively their being soaked in a flammable liquid, and an introduced flame or spark. These conditions might be present without a fire starting, but in the right combination they are jointly sufficient for it to do so. A lit match, an unextinguished cigarette end, a candle flame, friction between two suitable surfaces, is each sufficient to start the fire, but none is by itself necessary.

Thus it is that education is not necessary for someone to be a well-rounded, informed, richly alive person, but when it works as in the ideal it is intended to, it is sufficient for this: it can make it happen.

These thoughts can be tweaked in an interesting way by introducing another distinction, this time between instrumental and *constitutive* value. Instrumental value has a causative role in helping towards the attainment of something of higher value, while constitutive value is a component of a value, intrinsic or otherwise. Education causes you to be more knowledgeable, and being knowledgeable is valuable. Education is instrumentally valuable in your becoming so.

Knowing history or physics is a constituent of being knowledgeable, but it is not what causes you to be so, it *is* being so, a part or component of it.

Now the big question has to be asked: is there a single, overarching, supreme intrinsic value, or are there many intrinsic values? Yes, says the majority *vox pop*, there is an overarching intrinsic value, and they nominate 'happiness' as it, which means that all other values – all the other good things people appreciate and want – are instrumental to its achievement. Given that different things are appreciated and wanted by people in different degrees and combinations, it follows that they are instrumental, necessary conditions of the overarching value only relative to the combination that is sufficient to achieve it. For example, although money above a certain minimum quantum is a necessary condition of happiness for most people, there are some who do not regard it as necessary at all – although in practical terms someone has to be paying for the basics even if it is not themselves. Digging into this, one sees that whereas most people regard freedom from want as a necessary condition of happiness although not sufficient by itself to achieve it, there are some who regard freedom from the endeavour to get money as a greater necessity for happiness. The combination of the two explains why people buy lottery tickets.

As one would expect, some philosophers do not regard happiness as the supreme value. In regarding the four virtues of justice, wisdom, continence and courage as intrinsic values as the ancient Greek philosophers did, or compassion, continence and *ahimsa* as intrinsic values as Buddhists and

Jains do, happiness is not in the picture as any of an intrinsic, instrumental or constitutive value, although it might accrue as an epiphenomenon – a by-product – of living according to these values. Whether it does so or not is a matter of indifference. The question, 'Which would you rather be, a happy pig or an unhappy Socrates?', makes the point. It has to be granted, though, that the Epicurean and Stoic aim of achieving *ataraxia*, peace of mind, could be construed as happiness if, as is plausible, it can be identified with contentment.

These comments will immediately invite the charge that Aristotle, prince of the ethical theorists in Greek antiquity, made happiness the highest value to which all others are instrumental. This, however, is to rely on a wholly inadequate translation of his key term, *eudaimonia*, as 'happiness'.

'Eudaimonia' literally means 'good demon', a *daimon* not being a creature of malevolence in ancient Greek thought, but more like a spirit or (attaching the 'good' prefix 'eu' to it) an angel. So a state of 'eudaimonia' is the state of being *as if* looked after by a good angel. (Aristotle did not believe literally in good angels; he is employing a metaphor.) A better rendering of 'eudaimonia' is 'a flourishing state of well-being and well-doing'. A person living eudaimonically might feel happy, but this result is not the aim; the aim is to live eudaimonically because of what goes into doing so. For Aristotle, what conduces to eudaimonia is application of the most distinctive feature of human beings – namely, their possession of reason – to choices about how to act, selecting the middle path between opposing vices on a case-by-case basis. For example, courage is the middle path between cowardice and rashness; generosity is the middle path between meanness and profligacy – and so on. A person who lives the rational life is a eudaimonic person, a good person; his life is the good life. Its being or not being happy in the common acceptation of this term is not the point.

We might think of some people's lives being good in the sense that their effects on others are of great value even though they themselves suffered much to create that value. Someone might say that what we mean by describing their lives as good is 'that it was a good thing they lived', not that they themselves felt life to be good – how could they, for they suffered? But I think that if someone knew that what they were doing constituted a positive contribution, one perhaps of great significance to others, then even if they suffered and did not feel happy in the common sense of the term, they would know that their lives were good lives accordingly. This is another way that the idea of happiness as the greatest value can be contested.

In a discussion of this point round a dinner table someone might say: If happiness really were the greatest value, those who suffered as they did could be seen as consciously trying to promote a greater aggregate happiness that would outweigh their own individual unhappiness. This is a view that Utilitarians would take.

Someone else at the table might chip in with the thought that if a suffering person knew her suffering were promoting happiness elsewhere, it would make her happy too. This reflects a natural inclination to think that consciousness of good has to be positive in its effect on anyone to whom it occurs, and that there is a perfectly good sense in which one can say that such a consciousness is a happy one.

Both points can be granted; but it remains that it has also to be granted that someone could 'do the right thing' – the *right* thing always being so because it is a thing of value – though it made her deeply unhappy to do it. That makes any connection between happiness and achievement or instantiation of value a non-necessary one, surprising though that seems.

Stirring up all these considerations is intended to show that seeking what values and things we value to take from the past into the future, so that we can strive to ensure that we retain them despite what happens in the way of the dramatic changes portended by current trends, requires more thought than first appears. Apart from anything else, some of the things we have valued and currently value have contributed to problems that we hope the future will overcome. Out of the welter of considerations that arise, finding a way to identify with greater clarity what we wish to keep and to relinquish asks us to question more directly what the experience of mankind says about the matter. For this, the literature of utopia is a powerful guide. That is the subject of the next chapter.

8

UTOPIA

An AI-run world inhabited by transhumans is, in the eyes of the champions of both, a eutopia ('a good place'), but it is not a utopia ('nowhere') because it is already here or almost here. Earlier chapters recorded both the far-ranging, deep penetration of AI into so many dimensions of human affairs, and the fact that human beings are already transhuman in so many ways. The eutopian promise is that AI will generate wealth and at last realise the hope of technology, that it will liberate people either from the drudgery of labour or from labour itself, lifting the curse of Genesis that mankind must eat its bread in the sweat of its brow. Correlatively, transhumanism will liberate people from disease and a truncated lifespan, will enhance capacities for creativity and pleasure, will change – in positive ways, so the hope or implication is – the way life is experienced and lived.

It is remarkable how similar this vision is to that of eutopias dreamed up by people in the past, as this chapter will show. Surveying them illuminatingly displays what their writers saw as wrong with the world, and what they thought would be a better, or the best, state for humanity. From their descriptions of bad arrangements – dystopias – we see what they think eutopia should be; from the eutopias we see in their implied opposites what the writers condemned in the realities of life. This is material for thinking about what we should take from our past and present into the future.

But before making this survey it is well to heed a warning note, sounded by the question: at what cost might eutopia be achieved? What price, perhaps hidden, will be paid for entry, or (given that it is already happening) further entry, to this paradise? One is reminded of Ursula Le Guin's excoriating story, *The Ones Who Walk Away from Omelas.*[1] Omelas is a city where life is very good, indeed joyous: 'Joyous! How is one to tell about joy? How describe the citizens of Omelas?' The story begins with a description of a summer festival, illustrating the life of the 'bright-towered' city by the sea with its people relishing the pleasures of their existence. There are no soldiers, no clergymen, the city is free of strife and discord; all is a 'boundless and generous contentment, a magnanimous triumph felt not against some outer enemy but in communion with the finest and fairest in the souls of all men everywhere and in the splendour of the world's summer: this is what swells the hearts of the people of Omelas, and the victory they celebrate is that of life.'

But 'their happiness, the beauty of their city, the tenderness of their friendships, the health of their children, the wisdom of their scholars, the skill of their makers, even the abundance of their harvest and the kindly weathers of their skies', depend on a certain condition. The citizens know what this condition is, and by continuing to live in Omelas they signify their acceptance of it. The condition is that a child must be kept in a dungeon, suffering alone in fear, hunger and misery. 'The child used to scream for help at night, and cry a good deal, but now it only makes a kind of whining, and speaks less and less often. It is so thin there are no calves to its legs; its belly protrudes; it lives on a half-bowl of corn meal and grease a day. It is naked. Its buttocks and thighs are a mass of festered sores, as it sits in its own excrement continually.' When the citizens of Omelas reach a certain age they are taken to see this child through the bars of its dungeon. Whatever their sentiments on seeing it, they know that if the child were to be released, at that instant 'all the prosperity and beauty and delight of Omelas would wither and be destroyed. To exchange all the goodness and grace of every life in Omelas for that single, small improvement: to throw away the happiness of thousands for the chance of the happiness of one: that would be to let guilt within the walls indeed.'

However shocked the citizens might be on learning the condition on which they enjoy the bliss of Omelas, over time they come to think that if the child were released 'it would not get much good of its freedom' in the ordinary non-joyous version of Omelas that would result. It might get 'a little vague pleasure of warmth and food, no doubt, but little more. It is too degraded and imbecile to know any real joy'. And so the citizens reconcile themselves to the condition on which they and their city have their wonderful existence.

Le Guin then adds, 'But there is one more thing to tell.' Every now and then one of those taken to see the child does not go home afterwards, but instead walks down the street from the prison, and keeps walking; walks out through the city's beautiful gates, and on into the countryside; and keeps walking.

> Each alone, they go west or north, towards the mountains. They go on. They leave Omelas, they walk ahead into the darkness, and they do not come back. The place they go towards is a place even less imaginable to most of us than the city of happiness. I cannot describe it. It is possible that it does not exist. But they seem to know where they are going, the ones who walk away from Omelas.

The story can be read as a challenge to utilitarianism, which says that what is good is whatever promotes the happiness of the greatest number. On this theory, the contract made by the citizens of Omelas is justified, despite what it involves. For present purposes a different point is relevant. It is that achieving eutopia might require acceptance of something far from eutopian, tucked into the small print. What kind of thing might that be?

And what if there occurs, because of misapplications, misdirections, the escape of AI from human control, the unleashing of negative aspects of human nature by more intimate marriages between technology and the human body and brain? Then the already-arriving future is a dystopia, not a eutopia, perhaps irreversibly so.

Imagining eutopias has a long history, starting with the Golden Age myths in Hesiod and Homer. Later writers evidently came to think that it is depressing to place eutopia unreachably in the past, so they gave their imaginations to the future or alternative presents. Plato offered a picture of a rationally ordered society, his *Republic*, where philosophers rule, only the best are allowed to breed, and the resulting children are raised in state nurseries. The Roman historian Tacitus encouraged his readers to revive the austere republican virtues of Rome's earlier history by praising the hardy Germans who 'never weakened themselves by intermarriage with foreigners'. Christian authors, Tertullian chief among them, looked forward with glee to seeing non-Christians burn agonisingly in the flames of hell on Judgement Day. More peaceably and constructively, Tao Qian in early China dreamed of a perpetual springtime of peace and plenty, free from war and work.

The coming of modern times in Europe – the seventeenth and eighteenth centuries – imagined eutopias premised on the possibilities offered by the newly emerging sciences, or alternatively suggested by exploration's encounter with 'noble savages' whose simplicity of life reprimands European civilised decadence.

One paradigm of a eutopia is Voltaire's El Dorado in *Candide* (1759). Though paradigmatic, it leaves out two things typically a feature of eutopias, the weather and sexual ethics, eternal spring or summer and free love being typical requisites. As no mention is made of either, one has to assume both were agreeable. In passing, however, one notes that when Candide and his companion Cacambo are taken to have a bath they are assisted by 'twenty beautiful young virgins'. More interesting to the pair, which they learn as a result of the happy chance that Cacambo speaks El Dorado's language, is that the greed for riches and the vices it prompts are absent; gold, rubies and emeralds so abundantly litter the ground that the country's citizens take no notice of them. Delicious and copious banquets are provided free in palace-like public houses. A wise old man – who is 172 years of age – tells them that there are no priests and monks in the country, drawing from Cacambo the exclamation, 'What! Have you no monks among you, to dispute, to govern, to intrigue, and to burn people who are not of the same opinion as themselves?' Instead of bowing or prostrating themselves before the king when they meet him, Candide and Cacambo are advised to embrace him, which they do. There is no parliament, the king ruling benignly; there are no law courts or prisons, the populace not needing them because it is happy, untroubled, and plentifully supplied, so the country is crimeless. In the public squares, perfumed by cloves and cinnamon, fountains of rum freely play.

Because the two adventurers are of restless spirit, desirous to return to Europe (taking with them hampers full of the unregarded but glittering El Doradan ground-rubble), and in particular because Candide is anxious to be reunited with his *inamorata* Cunégonde, they request the king's permission to leave. After pointing out that they are ill-advised to quit so contented a place as El Dorado, the king says, 'Most assuredly, I have no right to detain you or any strangers against their wills; this is an act of tyranny to which our manners and our laws are equally repugnant; all men are by nature free; you have therefore an undoubted liberty to depart whenever you please.' And he orders that every help be given them to do so. El Dorado's interest in science and engineering is such that its talented savants are able to contrive safe passage for them, by means of ingenious machines, over the otherwise impassable mountains that protect El Dorado from the venal and corrupt outside world.

Voltaire's utopia differs from others prompted by the eighteenth-century Enlightenment's interest in tales told by explorers, in drawing on longer-standing reports of Spanish finds in South America, where gold and silver were abundant, and were shipped back to the Iberian kingdom to pay for its superpower status in the sixteenth century. But the Enlightenment imagination was inflamed into other utopian idealisations by encounters with 'noble savages'. A best-seller by the Comte de Bougainville describing his circumnavigation of the globe, *Voyage Autour du Monde* (1771), contains a description of Pacific Island communities and their ways that spurred Denis Diderot to write his *Supplément au voyage de Bougainville* (written in 1772, published 1796) which ignored the serious downsides of Pacific life noted by Bougainville, and concentrated instead on the sexual liberty of the natives he described.

As Bougainville's ship approached Tahiti it was surrounded by canoes full of naked nubile young women, who openly invited sexual congress. 'It was very difficult, amidst such a sight, to keep at their work four hundred young French sailors, who had seen no woman for six months', Bougainville writes; 'a young girl came on board ... and appeared to the eyes of all beholders such as Venus showed herself to [Prince Paris of Troy], having, indeed, the celestial form of that goddess. Both sailors and soldiers came to the hatchway, and the capstan was never hove with more alacrity than on this occasion'. Ashore, Bougainville thought he had been 'transported to the Garden of Eden ... fine fruit trees, intersected by little rivulets, keep up a pleasant coolness in the air ... A numerous people there enjoy the blessings which nature showers liberally down upon them. We found companies of men and women sitting under the shade of the fruit-trees, who all greeted us with signs of friendship'. Diderot's study of nature and the findings of the then new social sciences had convinced him that sexual energy, Eros, 'fuels the universe', and he leaped upon Bougainville's report to substantiate his claim that the reason for the happiness of the Tahitians was their being governed by nature, in contrast to the vice-prompting restrictions and formalities of French society in matters of sex and marriage.

Diderot's association with Jean-Jacques Rousseau had been close for a time, and he knew the latter's *Discourse on the Origin of Inequality Among Men* (1754) which extolled the virtues of mankind in its infancy, living in a state of nature, motivated only by humanity's innate goodness.[2] Although Rousseau never himself used the phrase 'noble savage', and although he identified the source of the corruptions of society as implicit in early man's first introduction of tools and fire which led to rivalries and *amour propre* (self-regard, self-interest), the idea that it is society and its sophistications that

142

corrupt human nature revived the notion of 'the ease of the golden age' (Bougainville's words anent Tahiti) and annexed it to 'primitive' life. I say 'revived' because whereas in antiquity the general belief was that humankind and its societies had long been declining from a superior remote past, Christianity had reversed the course of history's direction with the idea of a future paradisiacal goal, consisting in the Second Coming and the fulfilment of God's Kingdom.

In fact the idea of the 'noble savage' – or in Montaigne's far better rendering, 'nature's gentleman' – already had a long history. As already mentioned, Tacitus's book on the German tribes, published in 98 CE, praised their uncorrupted virtues, likening them to those of the first Romans of republican times. At this point nobility consisted in puritanical morality, not Dideronian freedom. The term 'noble savage' itself was coined by Dryden in his play *The Conquest of Granada* (1672); its hero Almanzor defends himself against a death sentence by asserting that he is no one's subject and therefore no one has a right to order his execution: 'I am as free as nature first made man/Ere the base laws of servitude began/When wild in the woods the noble savage ran'.

Perhaps the most detailed utopia produced in the Enlightenment is Louis-Sébastien Mercier's *L'an 2440* (*The Year 2440*) (1771), another best-seller of the age. It does not invoke a free and simple past but imagines an organised future. A Parisian wakes in 2440 to discover his city and its people transformed into a public-spirited, reason-governed community from which greed and vanity have disappeared. In anticipation of Haussmann's *grands boulevards* the streets are straight and wide, and mostly pedestrianised. A Temple of Clemency stands on the site of the Bastille. (Today a magnificent opera house does so.) There are no slums, the air is clear, fresh clean water bubbles from ubiquitous fountains, there is a score of hygienic new hospitals whose services are free to all. Malign institutions such as the Church, colonialism and slavery have been abolished. The press is uncensored, but authors are expected to promote virtue and aesthetic sensibilities in their readers. Everyone writes a book (somewhat as happens today, it seems) recording their best thoughts, which are read out at funerals in the place of headstones and monuments. Oddly, libraries are banned on the grounds that they are places of idleness, but a version of them remains in the form of repositories for theological and legal treatises, which are kept under lock and key, taken out only to be sent to other nations as a way of undermining them. In schools the classical tongues and history are not taught (because they record 'the disgrace of humanity, being crowded with crimes and follies'), the curriculum instead focusing on mathematics to instil rigorous thinking and physics so that nature can be understood. In the Enlightenment those who today would be called agnostics or atheists mostly settled for Deism, the view that, in default of any better explanation, the universe's existence must be attributed to a creative agency of some sort (but: where did *it* appear from? – they seemed not to have asked), even though Deists held that this agency has since lost interest or ceased to exist. Accordingly Mercier's schoolchildren are encouraged to peer through telescopes and microscopes to see the new universes thus revealed, but encouraged to honour the agency that brought them into being. Brought up to be reasonable and civic-minded, the future Parisians pay their taxes willingly and even donate more than their taxes to the arts and public well-being 'for love of the state'.

A notable lacuna in Mercier's account is equal rights for women. On the contrary, the New Parisians require that women be subservient and must not venture witty remarks, 'which men find annoying'. There is still punishment for crime, but the criminals co-operate in their punishment, some honourably choosing death, for which they are congratulated by the watching crowd.

Some of the characteristics of Mercier's futurist eutopia have their precedents in Francis Bacon's *New Atlantis* (1627, published after his death the year before). Its 'Bensalem' (which might look like 'Good Jerusalem' but it is derived from Hebrew and means 'son of peace') is a land of 'generosity and enlightenment, dignity and splendour, piety and public spirit', at the heart of which is a scientific research institute, 'Salomon's House', 'the very eye of this kingdom', dedicated to learning the secrets of nature and distinguishing between 'works of nature, works of art, and impostures and illusions of all sorts'. By contrast, Diderot's conception of a good society does not have precedents in the moral system of Bacon's New Atlantis; just the opposite. For in Bacon's utopia:

> there is not under the heavens so chaste a nation as this of Bensalem; nor so free from all pollution and foulness. It is the virgin of the world ... there is nothing amongst mortal men

145

more fair and admirable than the chaste minds of this people. Know therefore, that with them there are no stews, no dissolute houses, no courtesans, nor anything of that kind.

Bensalem is an island in the Pacific also, 'west of Peru', discovered accidentally by a European ship that had lost its way. The elevated moral character of the people is indicated by the fact that no public official accepts bribes. Since Bacon himself had fallen from his position as Lord Chancellor for accepting bribes, the detail is interesting. So is his sexual moralism, for Bacon was a practising homosexual (Aubrey in his *Brief Lives* says he was 'a pederast' and had 'ganimeds and favourites' aplenty) though he married, at the age of forty-eight, the fourteen-year-old Alice Barnham, daughter of a wealthy London merchant. She brought him the then large sum of £220 a year. It was a childless *mariage blanc*, undertaken no doubt for the income and as cover for Bacon's proclivities. It would not be unique in being so. There is nothing wrong with his being gay, though in the climate of his times it would not have been regarded as exemplifying the virgin purity of the Bensalemites.

Bacon's consuming passion was science and scientific discovery. He wrote extensively about scientific method, contributing thereby to philosophy and the advancement of science, his 'Salomon's House' being the inspiration for the Royal Society founded in 1662. In his day alchemy, magic, astrology, Hermeticism and the Kabbala were all the rage, their practitioners refusing to co-operate in order to keep their secrets to themselves in case they found the elixir of eternal youth and ways to transmute common metals into gold – eutopian aspirations.[3] Bacon advocated co-operation in scientific enquiry and experimental methods based on logical principles, to separate chemistry from alchemy, astrology from astronomy, medicine from magic, indeed all the natural from the occult sciences. His influence in this respect took some time to have effect; Isaac Newton later in the same century spent more time on mystical numerology and other occult endeavours than on the science that made him famous.[4]

Jonathan Swift's *Gulliver's Travels* (1726) is a classic eutopia-dystopia set of utopias. The sojourn of Lemuel Gulliver among the tiny Lilliputians, upon the shores of whose island he had been shipwrecked, reveals to him a people so obsessed with trivialities that they engage in hostilities with a neighbouring island state, Blefuscu, because the people there crack open their boiled eggs at a different end from the one that Lilliputians think right. When Gulliver helps Lilliput to victory over the Blefuscans by stealing the latter's navy, the Lilliputians demand that he help to subjugate them, but he refuses, so the Lilliputians condemn him to be blinded. He escapes before they can do it.

On his next sea-voyage Lemuel finds himself blown ashore on the west coast of north America, the land of the giant Brobdingnags. Found by a twenty-two-metre-tall farmer, he is put into the care of the farmer's daughter, Glumdalclitch ('little nurse' in the language of the land) and exhibited as a freak by the farmer for money. Eventually purchased by the country's queen, Lemuel is given a box – a miniature bed-chamber – in which he is carried about by Glumdalclitch whom the queen employs as his caretaker. In conversations with the country's king Lemuel describes Europe's ways, which disgust the king, especially the involvement of gunpowder, guns and cannons. Lemuel offers to show him how to make gunpowder but the king refuses on the grounds that its physical and moral consequences are too horrific. When Lemuel tells him about the society and politics of the English, 'our trade and wars by sea and land, our schisms in religion, and parties in the state', the king expostulates that they must be 'the most pernicious race of odious little vermin that nature ever suffered to crawl upon the surface of the earth'. In Lemuel's account of this episode he says that his 'colour came and went several times, with indignation, to hear our noble country, the mistress of arts and arms, the scourge of France, the arbitress of Europe, the seat of virtues, piety, honour, and truth, the pride and envy of the world, so contemptuously treated.' But later, on reflection, Lemuel decided that the king was right.

Brobdingnag's king was a philosopher (this word until recently comprehensively meant 'enquirer' and included 'scientist' in its designation), and on first encountering Lemuel thought he was a mechanical device – a robot. This detail brings to mind Descartes' visit to the hydraulic statues in the park at Saint-Germain-en-Laye outside Paris, which moved and spoke, giving Descartes the source of his thesis that all animals other than humans – who alone have souls – are automata. (To illustrate this theory Descartes once threw a cat out of an upstairs window, though how this proves anything is unclear.)[5]

Modern readers find Swift's account of the Houyhnhnms, a race of horses living on an island south of Australia, the most ambiguous of his examples, although it seems sincerely intended by Swift to be a eutopia. The Houyhnhnms are almost-passionless rational beings whose language completely lacks such terms as 'lying', 'power', 'government', 'war', 'law', 'punishment' and many more, as Lemuel discovers when he has learned enough about his hosts. They for their part think him a Yahoo, though a surprisingly superior one in comparison to the degenerate and disgusting wild monkey-like Yahoos infesting their country. His Houyhnhnm host, who treats him with kindness, is amazed and appalled by what Lemuel tells him about where he comes from. To his host's question about the causes of war, Lemuel replies that these:

> were innumerable; but I should only mention a few of the chief. Sometimes the ambition of princes, who never think they have land or people enough to govern; sometimes the corruption of ministers, who engage their master in a war, in order to stifle or divert the clamour of the subjects against their evil administration. Difference in opinions has cost many millions of lives: for instance, whether flesh be bread, or bread be flesh; whether the juice of a certain berry be blood or wine ... Neither are any wars so furious and bloody, or of so long a continuance, as those occasioned by difference in opinion, especially if it be in things indifferent. Sometimes the quarrel between two princes is to decide which of them shall dispossess a third of his dominions, where neither of them pretend to any right. Sometimes one prince quarrels with another for fear the other

should quarrel with him. Sometimes a war is entered upon, because the enemy is too strong; and sometimes, because he is too weak. Sometimes our neighbours want the things which we have, or have the things which we want, and we both fight, till they take ours, or give us theirs. It is a very justifiable cause of a war, to invade a country after the people have been wasted by famine, destroyed by pestilence, or embroiled by factions among themselves ... If a prince sends forces into a nation, where the people are poor and ignorant, he may lawfully put half of them to death, and make slaves of the rest, in order to civilize and reduce them from their barbarous way of living [this latter refers to colonialism].

Lemuel's Houyhnhnm host is revolted by the thought that 'a creature pretending to reason could be capable of such enormities'. When Lemuel explains money, avarice, the exploitation of the poor by the rich and how miserably the poor live in comparison, the vices of the aristocracy, and much else of no credit to his kind, his Houyhnhnm host observes that human beings' 'small pittance of reason' had been used only to:

aggravate our natural corruptions, and to acquire new ones, which nature had not given us; that we disarmed ourselves of the few abilities she had bestowed; had been very successful in multiplying our original wants, and seemed to spend our whole lives in vain endeavours to supply them ... That our institutions of government and law were plainly owing to our gross defects in reason, and by consequence in virtue; because reason alone is sufficient to govern a rational creature,

and that they were no better than the Yahoos of Houyhnhnm-land, who, if you threw among five of them enough food for fifty, would each set about trying to gather as much for himself as he could, fighting the others to do so.

Nowhere else in the *Travels* is so excoriating and accurate an account given of human folly and vice, as recounted by Lemuel to his Houyhnhnm host, most of it as true today as it was in Swift's time. Swift has Lemuel say that he admired Houyhnhnms to such an extent that he wished to remain among them always. The Houyhnhnms, 'endowed by nature with a general disposition to all virtues', had no conception of evil being possible for a rational creature; their 'grand maxim' was 'to cultivate reason, and to be wholly governed by it.' Their two principal virtues were friendship and benevolence; they 'preserved decency and civility in the highest degrees', and made no use of ceremony.

Temperance, industry, exercise, and cleanliness, are the lessons equally enjoined to the young ones of both sexes: and my master thought it monstrous in us, to give the females a different kind of education from the males, except in some articles of domestic management; whereby, as he truly observed, one half of our natives were good for nothing but bringing children into the world; and to trust the care of our children to such useless animals, he said, was yet a greater instance of brutality.

Amidst all this high-sounding rationality there are discordant notes, as the modern ear would hear them. The Houyhnhnms themselves are of two classes, superior and inferior, marked by the colour of their coats. The latter are servants, and eat less well than their masters. All Houyhnhnms practise eugenics in producing offspring, not just with a view to their fitness but to ensure that they are born with the right colour coat. 'They have no fondness for their colts or foals,' Lemuel says, 'but the care they take in educating them proceeds entirely from the dictates of reason.' Houyhnhnms couple for just as long as it takes to produce two offspring, one of each sex, and then part. If they have two of the same sex they swap one of them with another couple similarly placed.

Every four years the Houyhnhnms hold a grand assembly to discuss how everything is going and, if – which rarely happens – there is any problem, they rationally deal with it. At each assembly the only debate that ever divides opinion in their country is resumed: 'Whether the Yahoos should be exterminated?' Lemuel attends the assembly during his time there, and hears the arguments for getting comprehensively rid of so vile and degenerate a species, to which his own Houyhnhnm host responds that he has learned from Lemuel, his visiting more superior kind of Yahoo, an idea; to do what Yahoos do to their own Houyhnhnms in Lemuel's native land, which is to geld them. Castrating all young Yahoos will prevent them from reproducing so they will eventually die out, without the Houyhnhnms having to indulge in slaughter, and with the advantage that the gelded Yahoos will be more quiescent and manageable in the meantime.

At length Lemuel's Houyhnhnm tells him, with regret, that his fellows have persuaded him that either he must geld Lemuel in case he decamps to the Yahoos and leads them in a rebellion, or Lemuel must quit the country. Sick at heart, being so enamoured of Houyhnhnm society, and after many difficulties, Lemuel at last reaches England, where the smell even of his own family of Yahoos in London's Rotherhithe by the Thames so sickens him that he is unable to eat in their presence.

Sir Thomas More's *Utopia* (1516) gives its name to the genre, and is deservedly one of the most famous in it. It is much debated because of its ambiguity: did More really mean that he viewed the society described in the book as desirable, or, given that it contains much that More as a pious Catholic and heretic-hunter could not accept, did he intend it as ironic? One nineteenth-century commentator wrote, 'More hovers so perpetually on the confines of jest and earnest, passes so naturally from one to the other, that the reader is in constant suspense whether his jest be serious, or his seriousness a jest.'[6]

Utopia was written in Latin, which suggests that More did not wish it to be accessible to members of the general public who might be inspired by it to seek to replicate it in England's green and pleasant (for the rich) land. Instead it can be seen as an admonition to these same rich, and to questions of policy for addressing the abuses and inequalities in the England of his day, so that I, for one, do not buy the 'ironical' reading. But despite its first appearance in Latin, and its occasional learned references to classical authors, it became a sensation, being reprinted frequently not just in England but in France, Italy, Switzerland and Germany, and underwent translations into demotics, including English in 1551. In the front-matter of this last appears the note, 'A frutefull and pleasaunt worke of the beste state of a publyque weal', which represents *Utopia* as intended by More indeed to be a eutopia.

More's *Utopia* is an account given by a traveller called Raphael Hythloday – this awkward surname means 'teller of tall tales, purveyor of nonsense', adding to the 'irony' interpretation – of his five-year sojourn on the island of Utopia, a land of healthy, contented, civic-minded communists, where there is no poverty, and no exploitative and luxurious wealthy class. This is contrasted by Hythloday to the injustice of England, where landlords are evicting peasants from their lands by enclosures, to get more extensive pastures for their sheep, the peasants condemned thereby either to starvation or, if they steal in order to eat, to hanging. In *Utopia*'s first part Hythloday talks of the double injustice that this penalty for stealing is too severe, given that it is for a crime to which the thief is forced by hunger. If a man displaced from the land tries to beg he is imprisoned for vagabondage, and accused of wilful idleness when in fact he can find no work however hard he tries. As Hythloday waxes in this theme we see how directly More is addressing the contemporary socio-economic problems of England – price rises, the restricted supply of comestibles which 'causeth every man to keep as little houses and as small hospitality as he possible may' (*sic*), while those who still have means devote them to:

strange and proud newfangleness in their apparel and too much prodigal riot and sumptuous fare at their table. Now bawds, queans, whores, harlots, strumpets, brothel-houses, stews, and yet another stews, wine-taverns, ale-houses, and tippling houses, with so many naughty, lewd and unlawful games as dice, cards, tables, tennis, bowls, quoits – do not all these send the haunters of them straight a-stealing when their money is gone?

Hythloday recommends 'casting out these pernicious abominations' by passing a law requiring landlords to undo their enclosures and restore the farms and cottage industries they have destroyed – and if they will not obey, to dispossess them and redistribute the land to those who will. 'Suffer not these rich men to buy up all, to engross and forestall, and with their monopoly to keep the market alone as please them', he advises. What a modern ring this has.

The arrangement preferred by Hythloday and learned from the Utopians is, as indicated, communism. 'Wheresoever possessions be private, where money beareth all the stroke, it is hard and almost impossible that there the weal public may justly be governed and prosperously flourish; unless you think thus: that justice is there executed where all things come into the hands of evil men, or that prosperity there flourisheth where all is divided among a few … and the residue live miserably, wretchardly, and beggarly. Wherefore when I consider with myself and weigh in my mind the wise and godly ordinances of the Utopians, among whom with very few laws all things be so well and wealthily ordered that virtue is had in price and estimation, and yet all things being there common, every man hath abundance of everything.' And Hythloday commends Plato for thinking the same.

Asked to describe the land, people and customs of Utopia, Hythloday obliges, his account constituting the second part of *Utopia*, explaining how it is that the Utopians 'go beyond all the people of the world' in their 'good fashions, humanity, and civil gentleness'. He begins by saying that their land is well governed. A parliament meets annually in the capital Amaurote, each city or shire-town sending 'three old men, wise and well-experienced' as representatives. The city-dwellers rotate with the rural dwellers every two years so that all are practised in the crafts and skills of both. On the farms, hen's eggs are artificially incubated to ensure a regular and ready supply, which with the other products of husbandry are brought to the cities by land or water. At harvest-time men go out to the farms to help with the reaping. Utopia's king is elected from a group put forward by the people as most qualified to hold the office, and he reigns for his lifetime unless deposed 'for suspicion of tyranny', but all other public offices are held for a year only, except for the 'tranibores', the heads of the public offices, who are 'not lightly changed'. 'Nothing touching the commonwealth shall be confirmed and ratified, unless it have been reasoned of and debated three days in the council before it be decreed'. And matters of state cannot be discussed anywhere but in the council, on pain of death, 'to the intent that the prince and tranibores might not easily conspire together to oppress the people by tyranny and to change the state of the weal public.'

No one locks the doors of their houses because there is no crime, and every ten years people exchange houses. All city houses have gardens and the residents compete with their neighbours over who can do best at 'trimming, husbanding and furnishing' them. No one is allowed to be idle; everyone must work six hours a day, and all go to bed betimes. Rest periods during the working day are entertained by lectures, or music, or 'honest and wholesome communication'. Everyone wears plain homely clothes. The basis of social life is the family, consisting of large numbers of kindred. Daughters leave to be wives in other households but sons bring their families into the home. Every family is headed by the 'eldest and ancientest father' in it 'until he dote for age', whereupon the next eldest takes his place. Wives 'minister to their husbands, the children to their parents, and, to be short, the younger to their elders'.

The communism of the society is most clearly exhibited by its economic arrangements. Markets are distributed through each quarter of the towns and cities, where:

> every kind of thing is laid up in barns or storehouses. From hence the father of every family or every householder fetcheth whatsoever he and his have need of and carrieth it away with him without money, without exchange, without any gage or pledge. For why should anything be denied unto him, seeing there is abundance of all things and that it is not to be feared lest any man will ask more than he needeth? For why should it be thought that man would ask more than enough which is sure never to lack?

In any case most people eat in the common halls, where the food is free and well-cooked. Every meal begins with a reading of a text that 'pertaineth to good manners and virtue', but Hythloday adds that the reading is short so that 'no man will be grieved therewith'.

Large airy hospitals are provided, their size ensuring that 'the sick, be they never so many in number, should lie not too throng or strait' and should not infect each other. All efforts to cure the sick are made, and nurses sit by the permanently invalided to talk to them and keep them company. But incurables and those in great unrelievable pain are offered euthanasia, which is never forced on them but must be chosen voluntarily.

The Utopians make a point of inculcating contempt for money, gold, silver and gemstones. They do it among other things by decorating small children with these things, so that putting them aside on reaching a certain age shows that they are only childish toys. Iron is more useful and practical than gold and silver, and far more readily available; it seems folly to value gold and silver more highly. Utopians eat from earthenware and glass vessels, but make their chamber-pots out of gold, and from it too the chains and fetters that bind prisoners, thus applying it to the most unsavoury or contempt-inducing uses. When convicted, by the way, criminals are enslaved as punishment.

For the Utopians the highest good is 'pleasure, wherein they determine either all or the chiefest part of man's felicity'. But their pleasures are sober and decent ones, such as are 'good and honest'. And 'they judge it extreme madness to follow sharp and painful virtue'. True virtue is defined as living 'a life ordered according to nature', as reason tells us, for reason:

> stirreth and provoketh us to lead our life out of care in joy and mirth, and also moveth us to help and further all other, in respect of the society of nature, to obtain and enjoy the same ... if it be a point of humanity for man to bring health and comfort to man, and specially (which is a virtue most peculiarly belonging to man) to mitigate and assuage the grief of others, and by taking from them the sorrow and heaviness of life, to restore them to joy, that is to say to pleasure; why may it not then be said that nature doth provoke every man to do the same to himself?

Pleasure consists in health of body and, above all, in delights of the mind from reading and study.

Before couples marry they are presented naked to each other to be sure that there will be no physical repugnance when they wed. Hythloday says he laughed at this custom on first learning of it, until the Utopians pointed out its logic, saying that 'they do greatly wonder at the folly of other nations, which in buying a colt, whereas a little money is in hazard, be so chary and circumspect that though he be almost bare, yet they will not buy him unless the saddle and all the harness be taken off, lest under those coverings be hid some gall or sore; and yet in choosing a wife, which shall be either pleasure or displeasure to them all their life after, they be so reckless that, all the residue of the woman's body being covered with clothes, they esteem her scarcely one hundredth (for they can see no more but her face); and so do join her to them not without great jeopardy of evil agreeing together, if anything in her body afterward do offend and mislike them.'

The Utopians detest war, seeing in it nothing glorious as other peoples do, but nevertheless they exercise themselves in military disciplines, men and women alike, in case they are invaded and have to defend themselves, or see a neighbouring country being invaded or subjected to tyranny and they feel impelled to help. They accord glory to whoever can prevent war and bring about peace. This includes the expedient of bribing people in enemy states to assassinate their king, with smaller bribes for killing that king's advisers – though the reward is greater if the advisers can be captured and brought to Utopia, there to be bribed themselves to turn against the war – by these espionages averting war altogether. If hostilities still impend, the Utopians seek to hamper the enemy's war effort by sowing discord among his populace, supporting a rival for the throne there, and employing mercenaries to attack the enemy state.

In summing up Utopia, Hythloday reverts to its chief virtue, its communism, pointing out that where 'nothing is private, the common affairs be earnestly looked upon' – that is, people are civic-minded, pay attention to making things work, and play their part to promote the good.

Though no man have anything, yet every man is rich. For what can be more rich than to live joyfully and merrily without all grief and pensiveness, not caring for his own living nor vexed or

troubled with his wife's importunate complaints, not dreading poverty to his son nor sorrowing for his daughter's dowry? …
Therefore when I consider and weigh in my mind all these commonwealths which nowadays anywhere do flourish, so God help me, I can perceive nothing but a certain conspiracy of rich men, procuring their own commodities under the name and title of the commonwealth. They invent and devise all means and crafts, first how to keep safely without fear of losing that they have unjustly gathered together; and next how to hire and abuse the work and labour of the poor for as little money as may be.

And yet not even this brings the rich safety and satisfaction, for as a result of what they have done they find themselves living in a society polluted by 'fraud, theft, ravin, brawling, quarrelling, brabbling, strife, chiding, contention, murder, treason, poisoning' – all the things that 'die when money dieth'.

Though More is attacking the society of his day, as Swift attacked his own two centuries later, it is striking how similar the complaints are, how similar the proposed cure, and how relevant both the complaints and cures remain. The cure is justice applied by reason, and extraction from human affairs of the poison thorn of money. More was influenced by Cicero, Seneca, Plutarch and above all Plato, in particular Plato's own eutopia as set out in the *Republic*, whose governing philosopher-kings are to have no wealth in order to be free of its temptations, and no family in order to be free of partiality and the vulnerabilities brought by caring for some few above the rest in society. Like Voltaire's El Doradans, and like the historical Spartans by whose example More was also influenced, the residents of his Utopia eat together in public halls, reinforcing their communal – communist – life. This detail is the symbol for *sharing* which is the opposite of the private individualistic sequestration of resources practised by the rich, and which so many eutopian writers identify as the essence of dystopia.

The immediate reaction most would have to Hythloday's (and Lemuel's) nostrums is that human nature, which alongside its capacity for kindness and fellow-feeling contains too large a quantum of selfishness and aptness for jealousy, rivalry and hatreds, would undermine Utopian and Houyhnhnm society from the outset, as it would Plato's *Republic*. But two features of the argument in all three are that, first, when the temptations of money and the inequalities of status and luxury it buys are removed, and all things are held in common, a major source of selfishness and jealousy is removed likewise; and second, all three invoke education as the route to inculcating civic virtues required for the society to function. Well and good; but both equality and education are fragile solutions, for, in connection with the first, differences motivating jealousy and rivalry can easily arise from causes other than money, not least from within personal relationships, which are fruitful ground for trouble; and in connection with the second, education provides no guarantees – plenty of people are resistant to its effects, for any of many reasons, as any educator (the present writer included) will regretfully acknowledge.

In the late nineteenth and early twentieth century there was a surge of literary eutopias, among them a number of feminist ones. An example is Elizabeth Corbett's *New Amazonia*, which despite its author's socio-political commitments was published under the name 'Mrs George Corbett'. *New Amazonia* depicts a country run by women. The protagonist wakes from a hashish-induced dream to find herself in the year 2472. She is told that she is in Ireland, the population of which had long before been near-exterminated in a war with Britain, which repopulated Ireland with its own surplus women, women outnumbering men vastly because so many of the latter had died in the fighting. Because of the superior qualities of women the state that develops under their rule is eutopian. Although there are still men about, they occupy a subordinate status, not allowed to participate in state affairs because of the male propensity for 'corruption, injustice, immorality, and narrow-minded, self-glorifying bigotry'. (Fair point.) The government is known as 'Mother', and it is run by spinsters, married women not being allowed to hold office – presumably because of the malign influence of their husbands behind the scenes. Everyone is vegetarian, tobacco and alcohol are outlawed, euthanasia is practised on the disabled, lunatic and criminal. Female adulterers are condemned to manual labour, male adulterers are deported. There are strict immigration controls to keep out undesirables, the economy is state-run, Mother deciding what can be imported and manufactured.[7]

All the Amazonians are seven feet tall and live for centuries though never looking older than forty – they are all 'perfect models of beauty, grace and dignity' – a result achieved by a rejuvenation technology, administered in a luxurious spa, involving injection of the 'nerve force' extracted from dogs (which therefore die) into the veins of humans.

It is tempting to see Corbett's imagination as shaped by two principal influences, one being the way an ideal wife runs a Victorian household, this being a microcosm of New Amazonia in practically all details, and the other being what is regarded as a typical female desire to avoid ageing and appear beautiful, for which spas today provide treatments and unguents in quantity, as equal in their fatal effects on dogs and other experimental animals upon whom cosmetics are tested for safety.

In Charlotte Perkins Gilman's *Herland*, another feminist eutopia, there are echoes of similar themes, though the focus is different. Corbett was not much interested in motherhood *per se*, whereas in Herland it is the chief interest of the all-woman population. Being all-woman, reproduction is parthenogenetic and all the offspring are female. Herland is discovered by three men, who are captured by the athletic, dignified, rational women, whom the men find strangely sexless, and who indeed turn out not to be interested in sex. One of the men, after marrying one of the women and being denied fulfilment of his conjugal expectations, attempts to rape her, and is expelled from the country therefore. The population of Herland is controlled by limiting how many children each woman has. To ensure that all children are of good quality, any woman exhibiting bad character traits is made to forgo motherhood. They thus 'breed out, where possible, the lowest types', avoiding having 'an everlasting writhing mass of underbred people trying to get ahead of one another – some few on top, temporarily, many constantly crushed out underneath, a hopeless substratum of paupers and degenerates, and no serenity or peace for anyone, no possibility for really noble qualities among the people at large.'

The self-sufficiency of the Herlandians is exemplified not only by parthenogenesis but by the fact that though they have no cattle of any kind, they nevertheless have milk: their own. When it is explained to them that people elsewhere keep cows for milk, got by depriving the mother cow of her calf – which is taken away to be eaten – they are horrified. They are equally dismissive of religious ideas, not least that of eternal posthumous existence, which one of them, smiling her 'adorable, dimpling, tender, mischievous, motherly smile', describes as 'a singularly foolish idea. And if true, most disagreeable'.

The atheistical, virgin, virgin-birthing, calm, rational women of Herlandia devote themselves to learning, to raising the girls born to them not individually but by community effort, and to teaching them, the occupation of teacher being the most distinguished and honoured in the society.

Later feminism commends Gilman's Herlandia for its freedom from male domination and the kind of dysfunctional society men produce, for the control Herlandia's denizens have over their reproductive destinies, and for the recognition that what women do is work – contrary to the masculist trope that 'women stay at home and do not work', refusing to see that what happens at home is indeed work. But as always within any movement, and feminism is far from least in this respect, there are feminists who are critical; they accuse Gilman's 'separatist feminism' of perpetuating 'white feminism' and of tying women to their biology as their central feature.

One of the most thorough sets of proposals for how the world should be run, H. G. Wells' *A Modern Utopia* (1905), is eerily like an AI-run transhuman world without AI (but machines do most of the work) and without physical modification but instead a state-organised arrangement of human behaviour. As it is situated on a planet with a world government, the governors – the 'Samurai', an order of nobility – have satisfactorily met the challenge of maintaining a stable order through the implementation of dynamic social and scientific progress. Everyone on the planet speaks the same language and has the same laws and customs; they own their personal effects privately, but all natural resources are owned by the World State. The Samurai are ascetic Platonic philosopher-kings – Wells said that his idea was squarely based on the *Republic* – who by law must undertake a weekly hike in the countryside to keep their thoughts clear.

The people of Wells' Utopia are classed according to their qualities of mind. There are the creative Poietics, the practical and competent Kinetics, the unimaginative Dull, and the selfish and at best amoral Base. Men and women are equal, but a system of eugenics is practised in which marriage is only permitted between those who satisfy certain state-prescribed conditions. All are vegetarians, or rather pescatarians, there is no racism, and the chief animal companions of humans on

Earth – horses, cats and dogs – are absent from Utopia because they and their excretions are vectors of harmful infectious disease. People who do not fit in are exiled to islands and left to get on with life as best they can, deprived of state help. They tend to replicate dystopian practices such as are found back on Earth.

The book was influential; Samurai clubs were set up in London and elsewhere, and leading figures claimed it as shaping their views about how society should be organised (including William Beveridge, author of the Beveridge Report which, drawn up during the Second World War, was the blueprint for the welfare state and National Health Service in the UK). But it also invited sharp criticism for portraying an over-legislated one-party order in which freedoms are limited and which ignores the disruptive power of human greed and stupidity. Aldous Huxley's dystopian *Brave New World* (1932) was written as a rejoinder to it.

Summing up their themes and tendencies, one sees that the majority of utopias offered as eutopias by their inventors fall into two kinds. Both kinds serve as commentaries on the actual situation of humankind, for from them one recognises the all too familiar dystopian features of the real world. A typical eutopia is blessed by perennial good weather (warm springtime is a favourite) and an abundance of easily gathered, tasty – and usually vegetarian – food. There is no money, and in consequence there is no greed and therefore no strife, nor are there any (or at most, only a few) distinctions of social position. Reason governs. In many eutopias (especially if devised by men) sex is freely available. Criminality, if any such exists, is treated as an illness, and subjected to pleasant cures. People wear simple clothing, presumably made on looms at their cottage doors. If machinery exists it is not such as to despoil the natural environment, and its presence frees people to the gentle avocations of leisure and culture.

Another kind of eutopia, the minority sort, is more austere. This sort is not untypically exemplified by feminist imaginations. Sex, or at very least heterosexuality, has ceased to exist in them; eutopia is all-female, its population parthenogenetically renewed as in Herlandia. If men stray by chance amongst them they naturally fall desperately in love with one or more of the denizens, only to suffer some mortifying and humiliating comeuppance and to be expelled, with anathemas cast on their dystopic masculine instincts. It expresses the tragedy of humankind, and yet comes as no surprise, that in dreaming of better worlds so many writers have focused on remedies for the things that make the real world so often dystopian – poverty, inequality, labour, pain, disease, hardship, sexual privation, the absence of love. There is in this way much poignancy in eutopian visions, so eloquently identifying – by imagining their absence – the opposite of the ills plaguing reality.

More recent and contemporary utopias are indeed almost invariably dystopias; think of Huxley again and Orwell's *1984*. They express the sentiment that technology has proved to be more of a burden and a threat than a liberation and a help. Some of the horrors that earlier utopiasts sought to avoid in their eutopias, such as overpopulation and concentration of power in the hands of the greedy and wicked, have come to shape an image of a deeply troubled contemporary world in which science has extended humans' capacity for savagery almost beyond belief. Imagine plotting a graph to illustrate the change from Golden Age myths to today's anticipations of hells created by climate change, nuclear war, globalised epidemics, and worse, and the downward line would curve in the opposite direction to the upward curve showing technological development, forming an 'X' suggesting – as we remember from schooldays – 'Wrong Answer'.

Reflecting on Le Guin's Omelas prompts another unwelcome thought: that though life in the advanced economies of the world is not as blissful and easy as in that bright-towered city by the sea, nevertheless – relative to the condition of life for most people throughout history and many people in the 'Global South' today – in material terms it does not come far behind. And it does so on something like the same condition: the poverty and sweat-shop life of so many in poorer parts of the world. Take just one example: there is a town near Lagos in Nigeria where car batteries from the US are recycled; the lead from the process – saturating the air, lying in the dust on every surface in kitchens, schoolrooms, shops, absorbed by all who live there – poisons the town's population.[8] The chief implausibility in Le Guin's story is the absence of those negative facets of human nature that persistently, disruptively, simmer and roil in society, as if the naked cruelty towards the imprisoned little girl had concentrated and bled away all negatives in other relationships. But the condition – that the advantages of the citizens depend on the disadvantages of the little girl, taking her now as the representative of the world's immiserated – is the condition, or at least one of the principal conditions, on which today's advanced economies and their lifestyles rest.

Le Guin's eutopian Omelas is a dystopia. The lesson of all eutopias is that the real places inhabited by those who imagine them are dystopias, the negatives of which entail what the eutopian positives must be. Enthusiasts for superpowerful AI which integrates and manages the systems that run things, and finds solutions to problems, are seeking to overcome the inefficiencies of our systems – whether industrial, military, societal, or whatever – and what causes them, viz. the deficiencies in our knowledge and reasoning, our skill, our energy, our resources of time and money. Likewise transhumanists aim to do away with the negatives of our inherited biology, its proneness to injury and disease, its low levels of strength, its perceptual and cognitive limitations, its insufficient degree of longevity, and more. What is the condition – the imprisoned little girl – in these aspirations?

In both the condition is: the abandonment of human existence as we still know it. For the tech eutopiasts this of course is the very point, the desideratum; for them it represents liberating the little girl from her dungeon to romp with her fellows among the bright towers by the sea. There is a fundamental question for anyone who, while acknowledging the wonders and prospects offered by AI and transhumanism, is curious to know whether, in the small print, a less congenial condition yet lurks. As the next chapter suggests, there well may be.

An AI-run world and transhumanist modification of the people in it are eutopian projects aimed at achieving many of the desiderata identified in utopian writings. They are not unusual in being so; every initiative designed to counter the world's ills is eutopian in this sense. For example, the increasing dominance of capitalism in the Eurocentric world since the eighteenth century prompted a variety of theories and movements in response, from communism through socialisms of different kinds to anarchism, some as alternatives to capitalism and others offering a spectrum of ways of managing it, from mixed-market social-democratic arrangements to letting it fulfil its logic so completely that the problems it causes will be overcome by its sheer success, which is what is promised by the anarchism of libertarian thinking. But each is about a better way, a better future; some even promise paradise, and it is interesting that this is a feature shared by the furthest reaches of left-wing and right-wing thinking respectively.

9

BACK TO THE FUTURE

First among all other valuables we should wish to carry into the future from our humanity-constituting past is something so fundamental that we would only realise its importance by losing it. It lies at the centre of so much of what makes humanity *human*, for both good and ill, that attempting to overcome the ills it causes, and the ills inflicted upon it by external factors, requires changing both the condition of human life and the physical and psychological character of human beings – respectively, by delegation to AI systems of what people and their societies *do*, and by transhumanist bodily and psychological modification of what people *are*. Both therefore are challenges to the fundamental thing I argue we should wish to carry from our cumulative past into tomorrow. If the changes wrought by an AI-run world and increasing transhuman development represent the end of humanity as it is now and has emerged since the arrival of *Homo sapiens* on the planet, then it is not *we* who inhabit the future, but successor creatures, so it is not *our* tomorrow we are thinking of, but the abandonment, the end, of our today and yesterday. As remarked more than once, there are some who think this would be a good thing. And sure enough, there is plenty about today and all our yesterdays that we would like to get rid of. But curiously, most of these 'some' envisage themselves (in a crucial sense of them*selves*) as occupying, witnessing, enjoying the hoped-for benefits, of living among the successors of humanity. I wonder whether they see an inconsistency here. For this signals the point I wish to make.

The fundamental thing I argue that we should wish to carry into tomorrow is what I shall call the *essential self*. It is a concept rich in meanings and implications; to explain it requires some unpacking. It is the location of values, and carries all of them with it. It is to be contrasted with what I shall call a *nominal self* as what, for example, a chatbot like ChatGPT is, an AI system which *presents* as a person, an interlocutor, with which one can talk, or more accurately 'talk', as if it were another self like oneself, mimicking a human self in the encounter – the 'relationship' – which is already such (and the technology is advancing with great rapidity) that the mimicry of selfhood or personhood in chatbots, for example in virtual girlfriends and boyfriends and as therapists, has led to many feeling that they are in a genuine relationship with the bot as with a mind. And this to such a degree that people act on bots' advice, even their urgings – to the point of committing suicide in some tragic cases.[1]

Here are some of the things we associate with the subjectivity of a human self: experience, feeling, empathy, concern, interest, dislike, passion, fear, hope, purpose, desire, shame, grief, suffering, pain, joy, exaltation, happiness, achievement. Much more could be added to the list. In human-to-human relationships, even transient ones as in speaking with a shopkeeper or taxi driver, what one gets is recognition as a being to whom attribution of these features of subjectivity would be normal. Ask a question of such a being, and one gets an answer.

Contrast this with what one gets in encounters with bots. One does not get answers but responses from a bot; not recognition but categorisation. The bot does not have experience but data. A human interlocutor is questioned, a bot is prompted. What happens in the thoughts and feelings of a human being is subjective, what the AI running a bot does is objective in sampling the data in its large language model (LLM; perhaps by the time this book is published it will be 'dragon hatchling' architecture or its successors even more powerfully at work, but this is a difference of degree not kind). A bot is not concerned or emotionally engaged even to the slightest degree, but indifferent; it is not interested but both disinterested and uninterested in the literal sense of these terms. Likewise in the most literal sense, AI is AI, *artificial* intelligence; it mimics the appearance of a few of the subjective states listed, but only mimics them. Accordingly, what happens between a human and a bot is not relationship but interaction.

After delving into the concept of selfhood and the contrast between essential and nominal selves, this chapter will return to the ambitions of those who wish to see AI operating to shape most or all aspects of society, and those who promote further transhumanisation, the two obviously connected. As regards the latter, resources for thinking about their implications will come from familiar places: to consider worst-case scenarios, Frankenstein, Terminator and the Matrix will prompt a few thoughts; the human (or, some transhuman and some human) species in Aldous Huxley's *Brave New World* will do the same; on the transhuman aspiration for longevity the arguments in the final scene of Karel Čapek's *The Makropulos Secret* will be considered, together with the social and economic consequences of transhuman/human populations living very long lives. And there will be some questions asked that the protagonists of ultratech future speculations seem not to ask, for example: Elon Musk envisages downloading his mind to a computer with the prospect of uploading it again to a new brain (in a new, young, fit and beautiful body presumably, rather as Saint Paul imagined the resurrected dead at the Last Trump); but does this mean that the computer storing Elon's mind is Elon? Will it be a thinking thing, a person, the person Elon Musk? If so, switching it off would be murder. But if any AI system running on a computer network were to achieve essential selfhood – consciousness, intention, self-awareness – switching it off would be murder too. What are our moral obligations to AIs? To bots?

The starting point for all these considerations is the idea of the 'self' itself – not, it is vital to note, for selfish, solipsistic or narcissistic reasons, but because only if there are *other* essential selves with which any one such can enter into a relationship, the very idea of *values worth carrying into the future* becomes moot, given that all the values most central to human existence are predicated on what essential selves are and do. This recalls the striking concept of *Ubuntu* in Bantu value-systems, 'Ubuntu' meaning 'humanity', encapsulated by 'I am, because you are'.

First, then, here are some considerations about selfhood.[2]

The literary critic Harold Bloom, no stranger to hyperbole, credited Shakespeare with 'the invention of the human' in being 'the first' to recognise the identity of the self through time and the uniqueness of personality. This is of course a piece of rhetorical nonsense. The literary evidence available from that *Ur*-work of literature, the Epic of Gilgamesh, over four thousand years ago, to Shakespeare's own Renaissance epoch, tells us otherwise, to say nothing of what literature, philosophy and the sciences both natural and social have since had to say. Grant Shakespeare his brilliant exploration of personhood and its interiority in his characters and their soliloquies, but think of all the evidence for the same awareness in literature from the earliest advent of literacy. Consider the grief of Gilgamesh for Enkidu, so like that of Achilles for Patroclus in *The Iliad*, and reflect on what it shows: an acute individuating awareness of self and other, the tie between them, the meaning of the tie's severance by the other's disappearance from the world. Each hero's loss is profoundly felt as *intensely* personal and yet relational, cutting to the heart of himself and threatening to engulf him in the loneliness of his loss – the loss of engagement with another self. Their grief is wholly familiar to anyone who has experienced grief, closing the gap of time and culture completely. It is not possible to understand the nature of grief without having the concepts of individuality, personhood, and their setting in the narrative of life.

As we have seen, in the schools of philosophy in ancient Greece and Rome a persistent theme, common to Epicureans, Stoics and others, was the aim of achieving *ataraxia*, inner stability and peace of mind, in the midst of life's vicissitudes. For the Epicureans, the route to *ataraxia* was a choice of setting and practice, in the form of a withdrawal to a 'garden', a place apart shared with others of like mind. For the Stoics it was development of strength of character, management of one's response to assaults from without, and one's mastery of what is within such as appetites, desires and fears. For both Epicureans and Stoics the choice is made by a self about how things are to be for itself.

If yet more evidence were needed, one could cite Sophocles' *Oedipus at Colonus* in which the tragic blind king tells his daughter Antigone that 'three masters – pain, time, and the nobility in the blood – have taught me patience', or the poems of Ovid and Horace, the former portraying the experience that anyone in any era has in the privacies of intimacy, the latter meditating on what matters in life as surveyed from the vantage of retirement from its public stresses and thereby returning fully to contact with oneself. Conscious selfhood and its setting in personal histories are the pivots on which these writings turn. Chaucer's Canterbury pilgrims, Petrarch thinking of Laura, Dante thinking of Beatrice, are all vividly self-aware, as one typically is in the experiences of love and loss, in both of which it is not only the burning awareness of self but of another individual self, and its meanings for oneself, that are central.

Above all, think of Montaigne, explorer of selfhood *extraordinaire*. His greatest successor in the art of the essay, William Hazlitt, said, 'Montaigne was the first to have the courage to say as an author what he felt as a man.' There is no neater specification of what is special about Montaigne, not least the frankness of his self-revelation, his lack of pretension and conceit, and his generous though amused view of human existence.

Montaigne was fascinated by all things human, and writing about it was his meditation upon it. He had resigned from public life as a magistrate in the Parlement of Bordeaux to devote himself to leisurely study, but instead of leading to the expected Horatian idyll of self-cultivation, inactivity and idle reading gave him a nervous breakdown. He cured himself by writing about humanity in the form of one specimen of it, viz. himself.

> When I lately retired to my own house, with a resolution, as much as possibly I could, to avoid all manner of concern in affairs, and to spend in privacy and repose the little remainder of time I have to live, I fancied I could not more oblige my mind than to suffer it at full leisure to entertain and divert itself, which I now hoped it might henceforth do, as being by time become more settled and mature; but I find that, quite contrary, it is like a horse that has broke from his rider, who voluntarily runs into a much more violent career than any horseman would put him

to, and creates me so many chimaeras and fantastic monsters, one upon another, without order or design, that, the better at leisure to contemplate their strangeness and absurdity, I have begun to commit them to writing, hoping in time to make it ashamed of itself.

Since he was neither a military man nor a man of affairs, Montaigne's only subject was himself; so he resolved to try (*essayer*) to assay himself, his nature, his opinions, his attitudes and reactions, pretending nothing and confessing all. 'I am myself the matter of my book,' he wrote:

> others form Man; I give an account of Man and sketch a picture of a particular one of them who is very badly formed and who, if I could, I would truly make very different from what he is; but that's past recalling … every man carries the entire form of human condition. Authors communicate themselves to the people by some especial and extrinsic mark; I … by my universal being; as Michel de Montaigne, not as a grammarian, poet, or lawyer.

His great question was Socrates' question: 'how should one live?' and this makes him a contemporary for all times. Scholars like to emphasise the respects in which he was of his own time, positioning their interpretations of him in the turbulence of Renaissance and Reformation that made it possible for him to write as a pagan while in the midst of the sixteenth century's bitter Wars of Religion. His own family were divided between the Protestant and Catholic causes, but, though following the example of Justus Lipsius by remaining scrupulously orthopractic to outward view as a Catholic, every indication in his writings is that he was a sceptic in religion as in everything else, and had – as Pascal critically noted – a pagan attitude to death as the end of personal existence. But when his readers recognise his universality they see why he speaks with equal clarity to his contemporaries at the end of the sixteenth century, to Voltaire in the eighteenth century, to William Hazlitt in the nineteenth, and to readers today.

The two keys to Montaigne are his sympathetic imagination, and his scepticism. He recognised that understanding human nature and the human condition is crucially a matter of entering sympathetically into the experience of others, which means, crucially, encountering the essential self of others.

I am one of those who are most sensible of the power of imagination: everyone is jostled by it, but some are overthrown by it. It has a very piercing impression upon me ... I could live by the sole help of healthful and jolly company: the very sight of another's pain materially pains me, and I often usurp the sensations of another person. A perpetual cough in another tickles my lungs and throat.

His scepticism is inspired by the ancient Greek philosopher Pyrrho of Elis. Pyrrho argued that because the arguments for and against any proposition are equally good or bad, one must suspend judgement. This open-minded, non-committal, often ambiguous stance suited Montaigne. He accordingly chose as his motto *Que sais-je?*, 'What do I know?' said with a

Gallic shrug. But there is a nuance here well discerned by the scholar Pierre Villey: that Montaigne was a true Pyrrhonian only in his middle period – the period of Book Two of the Essays. In Book One he was a Stoic, that is, one who believes that we must, as noted above, resign ourselves with courage to face life's inevitabilities, but must master what lies under our own control: our appetites, fears and desires. By the time of Book Three, written a decade later, Montaigne had come to accept what the Chinese philosopher Mencius before him, and Rousseau after him, independently believed: that man is naturally good.

The Romantics of the nineteenth century found Montaigne too dispassionate, too cool, in contrast to their style of enthusiasm. But those who had learned enough from life to understand the saying 'in youth I loved Ovid, in age I love Horace' well understood his point. Stefan Zweig was one; before his suicide in 1942 Zweig listed the general propositions that Montaigne, contradicting his sceptical *acatalepsia* (the inability to come down definitively on one view), nevertheless came to assert as convictions, all on the theme of freedom: freedom from vanity, from partisanship, from ambition, from the fear of death. Montaigne assumed the role of detached spectator of the human comedy, and advised having a private 'room behind the shop' as he put it – rather like Virginia Woolf's 'Room of One's Own' – where one could commune with oneself in peace and solitude. This, he said, was a necessary condition for exploring humanity by exploring oneself. From awareness of one's essential self, one comes to appreciate its constitutive role in others.

But although Montaigne extolled the virtues of solitude, he also advised conviviality and friendship, and the profound lifelong love he felt for the friend he lost early in life, the poet Étienne de la Boétie, demonstrates that he understood this on his pulses. That is an attractive feature of the man, and goes a long way to explaining the ingenuousness, modesty and sanity of his account of himself as a self-portrait of humanity; for it is not possible to know oneself without knowing others, any more than one can know one's own country properly without having travelled abroad.

Montaigne could, with a tinge of mischief, illuminate one idea by a very different idea. Thus, talking about how our desires and ambitions are augmented by the difficulties we encounter in pursuing them, he invokes the example of ancient Sparta's lawgiver, Lycurgus, who made it a rule that married couples should behave like secret adulterous lovers:

> To keep love in breath, Lycurgus made a decree that the married people of Lacedaemon should never enjoy one another but by stealth; and that it should be as great a shame to take them in bed together as committing with others. The difficulty of assignations, the danger of surprise, the shame of the morning, these are what give the piquancy to the sauce ... Pleasure itself seeks to be heightened with pain: it is much sweeter when it smarts and the skin is rippled. The courtesan Flora said she never lay with Pompey but that she made him wear the prints of her teeth. And so it is in everything: difficulty gives all things their estimation.

There are significant points to take from Montaigne's views, so lightly and passingly expressed, for the idea of the essential self and its constitution by encounter with other selves. Contrary to Bloom's assertion, this and all the preceding examples predate Shakespearean soliloquy. After Shakespeare (but not because of him) the question of the self looms even more explicitly into view. One example is afforded by Spinoza's theory about human freedom in the final book of his magisterial *Ethics*, which is that it is achieved by bringing into the clear light of thought those subconscious, half-formed, often error-strewn thoughts and feelings that hinder us in our lives and make us struggle. The anticipation of Freudian psychoanalysis and other forms of psychotherapy is obvious. The subject of this process is the self, the self in bondage (Book IV of the *Ethics* is titled 'Of Human Bondage') and the self liberated (Book V is titled 'Of Human Freedom').

Spinoza was writing in the mid-seventeenth century; later in that century John Locke published his *Essay Concerning Human Understanding*, sending copies to philosophical colleagues to ask whether he had left anything out. One, William Molyneux of Dublin, replied that he had neglected to discuss the question of what makes a person the same person over time, from birth to death: the principle of personal identity. In the second edition of his *Essay* Locke included a new chapter to take account of this theme. His argument there is that what connects a person to his past is memory; one is the same person as he to whom the experience occurred that laid down the memory, but if memories are lost – as for example by a head injury – one is no longer the same person that one was; identity over time has been interrupted and thereby lost. This suggestion was immediately attacked, first by theologians who invoked the idea of the soul as the principle of individuality and identity (moreover, identity from the time of the soul's creation onward to the rest of eternity), then by other philosophers who pointed out that a memory can only count as a memory if the rememberer is the same person, by some *other* principle, in the first place. Moreover the idea that loss of memory is loss of identity seemed absurd: the small boy who steals apples is continuous with the courageous young soldier who wins a medal, and he in turn with the gouty old general complaining of the world in an armchair at his club, but the gouty old general may well have forgotten stealing apples in childhood, conveniently or otherwise.

A vigorous debate about personal identity consumed 'the wits of the kingdom' ('wit' once meant 'intelligence', not a capacity for spontaneous jokes) to such an extent that in 1712 the *Spectator* magazine published a demand for all the kingdom's wits to get together to determine what it truly is. The furore inspired the 'Tory Wits' – John Gay, John Arbuthnot, Lord Bolingbroke and others – to combine together to produce a satire called *The Memoirs of Martinus Scriblerus*, the eponymous hero being a superficial, futile but enthusiastic dabbler in all matters intellectual. In one of the chapters – trigger warning: this would not pass muster in today's world, quite rightly – he runs off with a pair of conjoined twins exhibited in a travelling circus, for he has fallen in love with one of them, the other perforce having to go along in the elopement. The circus owner is furious, because the twins were lucrative for him. So he brings a legal case against Martinus, accusing him not merely of theft and kidnapping but (here the trigger is pulled) of committing incest, adultery and fornication with his sister-in-law every time he and his wife enjoy their conjugal mutualities, because the twins are joined 'at the organ of generation'. The opposing barristers in court argue the question whether the twins are one person or two, rehearsing the arguments over personal identity in the process.

The matter would have been settled if, three decades later, on the publication by David Hume of his *Treatise of Human Nature*, everyone agreed with his view that there is no such thing as the self, at least in the sense of The Self. Hume took this view because, he said, if you introspect – look within yourself – to see what there is over and above, behind, alongside or embracing all your occurrent sensations, perceptions and thoughts, which is The Self that (like some sort of a receptacle) contains all these things, you will find nothing of the sort. The self, small-s, is just the bundle of sensations, perceptions and thoughts happening at the moment. Hume thought this because, as an empiricist, he held that an idea can only have real meaning if there is an empirical experience that gives rise to it. But because there is no empirical experience of A Self alongside and separate from occurrent experience, the idea of it is empty.

Hume said that his *Treatise* 'fell dead-born from the press' on publication; no one read it, not even the one person who reviewed it. It later became a philosophical classic, but not even then did his theory of the self persuade. Rather the contrary; as the classicism of the eighteenth-century Enlightenment yielded to the Romanticism of the nineteenth century, the idea of the self became even more significant. Whereas the ancients had thought a 'genius' was like a little spirit that perched on your shoulder and breathed inspiration ('in-spiration' literally means 'breathing in') into your ear, the Romantics assimilated genius right into the self; its poets and composers did not *have* a genius (sitting on their shoulders or anywhere else) but *were themselves* geniuses. Think of Swinburne's 'I am that which began/Out of me the years roll/ Out of me, God and man' as a motto for the universal centrality of the self, the maker of the world not just within but around.

And that brings us to Freud and Jung, to a multiplication of selves – subconscious, unconscious, conscious – and the branching implications of these ideas, not least among them the privileges, the inviolabilities, the claims, the aversion to affronts, the development, nurturing, discovery, individualism, uniqueness, of selfhood: 'because I'm worth it', as the advertisement has it. Give the label 'the consumerist self' to this latter phenomenon to distinguish it from what is meant by 'the essential self'. The consumerist self requires appurtenances to constitute and affirm selfhood, in the express form of 'to own is to be'. It is, however, itself arguably a form of quest for the essential self, the thing sought – when life's distractions and anxieties complicate or even block a secure sense of essential selfhood – by people who solicit the help of counselling or psychotherapy, or conversely seek to escape what they are afraid to find there by means of drink, drugs or frenetic aversion activities. This is a natural feature of what anyway impresses upon us a sense of selfhood, namely – as the word 'impress' literally tells us – what comes from without in encounters with the world and others. A telling example is what Helen Keller relates in her *Story of My Life* of the vividness of touch and smell in encountering the living natural world, and even more so of her mother's embraces, feeling with her fingers her mother's face and lips as her mother spoke, and the communication learned from her teacher Anne Sullivan by spelling words onto each other's hands. The Keller story is remarkable because what would have been a barren interiority, at best, without rich input from outside, sprang from that input all the more intensely into life precisely because of all that was *other* relative to it.

A reader might long since have paused, as these foregoing remarks unfolded, to entertain a sceptical thought. This is that the idea of an essential and therefore by implication *unitary* self lying within each of us, at the core, seems to be controverted by the actual experience of selfhood, which is that most if not all people do not appear from outside or even to themselves to consist of a single self, in just one clearly defined referent in each case of the pronoun 'I', but in a number of selves projected to the world – to different people, in different circumstances. Even inwardly, introspectively, to themselves, different selves seem to manifest depending on mood and the prevailing condition of life at a given point. Many people engage in constant or at least frequent efforts to modify themselves, or to develop a dominant self that will master other but self-betraying selves they find within – the self-betraying selves that cannot concentrate, sleep, combat fears, face realities, maintain the discipline to persist in reaching a goal. In this regard it would seem that one's question is not 'Who am I?' but 'Which am I?' – 'Which am I *really?*'

The response to this is to adjust the question yet again to 'What am I?' *qua* an entity with a continuing presence at the centre of a life in relationship with others and a circumambient world. Thus put, the answer invited can acknowledge the variability of mood and the way that one relates to others and circumstances with different aspects of oneself – how we behave with a close friend and how we behave in a formal interview will be selected (whether consciously or otherwise) as the face best suiting the occasion. But they are *aspects*, faces, of something that underlies all of them, which manifests clearly enough in thinking about (or having feelings about) such encounters when alone afterwards.

Crucially, knowing that other selves have the same kind of manifestations-to-self is what makes us adjust to whichever manifestation of oneself one presents to them – what effect on them one wishes to have or to avoid. This brilliantly illuminates what is at issue: we do not worry about hurting the feelings of a chatbot, or wishing it to like us or have a good opinion of us. And that is because the simulacrum of a self – a nominal self, an imitation self – manifested by a bot in its algorithmically-tailored responses to prompts is not of something in a relationship with us but merely in an interaction with us. Ask what we think about the difference between having a relationship with another person of the kind one does when, say, considering marrying that person, and a relationship with the kind of AI companion-(and probably sex-)robot already or soon on the market. Suppose such a robot is practically indistinguishable from a human person physically, and virtually indistinguishable in apparent psychology (if not wholly so, apart from its endless tractability): is a relationship with it the same as, as good as, as meaningful as, better than, a relationship with another human being? If not, why not? If better, in what way or ways? To reply that it is not as good and meaningful is to acknowledge that the value of relationship lies in its being an engagement with an essential self – another essential self – connecting with one's own.

This is not to deny that having an AI, bot or robot companion might have advantages for some; it could be better than talking to oneself (or doing other things by oneself). It is imaginable that some might like having a companion which can be put back in the cupboard when not needed – which is a burden only on the electricity bill, and unless programmed to do so does not challenge or answer back, but only serves and affirms. Intuition AI's ElliQ robot provides 'emotional support, cognitive stimulation, and health and wellness assistance to older adults', and Japan is investing in the technology for the same purpose.[3] A 2025 survey in the US found that 52% of adults have used chatbots and 38% believe that chatbots can form deep relationships with them. Research by Intuition AI, whose ElliQ is a small device on purpose designed *not* to look human in order to avoid deceiving people, is not a mere

189

responder to prompts but is proactive, initiating nearly two-thirds of the interactions with their users, remembering conversations, engaging and encouraging activity. It works; 97% of users report health improvements, 94% feel less lonely, 90% an overall improvement in quality of life, and 88% feel more in touch with the world in general.[4] These are impressive indications of the positive uses bots can have. Every passing week sees increased capability in the technologies involved. In circumstances in which populations are ageing and not yet sufficiently transhuman in the devices and prosthetics they already have – artificial joints, pacemakers and the like – assist-bots are an obvious boon. And so they might be too for the epidemic of loneliness in advanced economies, and for much besides.

Well and good: but now consider some further questions, and some potential downsides. This involves going to the far end of possibilities once regarded as science fiction but now here or within reach. Suppose the day arrives when one can connect a chip in one's brain (brain–chip interfacing is already here) to a computer and be fed experiences of a world created by the computer. Imagine that one could stay in that world – perhaps one is permanently in bed, connected to tubes providing nourishment and removing waste, and to electrodes that stimulate muscles sufficiently to prevent physical deterioration. (This is not essential to the example; like one of those 'bed rotting' youths one could bestir enough to collect a food delivery at the front door and go to the toilet.[5]) Given that the majority of people would rather be fed a eutopian virtual reality than a dystopian one, existence in this

Matrix-like manner would be happy. If happiness, *qua* emotional state, is the highest good, then this is the way to go. What, after all – many might ask – is so good about 'real life' anyway, with all its troubles and difficulties? In reply, one notes that (at time of writing) as people are in increasing numbers leaving dating apps to return to In Real Life ('IRL') ways of meeting potential partners, and as the social media space in general is seeing significant numbers leave and bots increasingly taking over, it would seem that even the negatives of being IRL are preferable to at least many others. One way to sharpen the point about the value of virtual as opposed to real experience is via the question and its implications, asked in an earlier chapter, 'Which would you rather be, a happy pig or an unhappy Socrates?'

Reflecting on a society full of nominal selves, the dystopic possibility of Frankenstein's 'monster' comes to mind. This is not as apt an example as one might think, if one reads the exchange between the 'monster' and Frankenstein in the snowy wastes where the former begs the latter to provide him with a companion, recreated from corpses like himself, with whom, far from human habitation, he could live without the agony of loneliness and rejection. He desires another self – another essential self – to be in relationship with. Frankenstein's refusal appears cruel, his disgust and horror at what he has produced overriding any feelings for the humanity as palpable in the 'monster's' hunger for companionship as in his desire for revenge on his maker for the hideous reality of his existence. In popular imagination, however, Frankenstein's 'monster' has come to represent a monster indeed, like one of those cinematic zombies who menacingly stagger about with the sole intention of killing people. Employing this trope, and invoking the much more apt *Terminator* movie franchise, turns our gaze towards what could happen if AI and AI military and police robots go wrong, escape human control, and get ideas of their own, plausibly premised on the fact, for fact it is whatever else one wishes to say, that human beings are a very pesky species whose wars, greed, cruelties and environmental depredations are shown so well by Swift and other utopiasts.

Leaving aside the intriguing question whether Elon Musk considered the name 'Skynet' before choosing 'Starlink', one recalls that the *Terminator* movies portray cyborgs at war with the human Resistance to Skynet's efforts to wipe them out. 'Judgment Day' is the day Skynet becomes self-aware and destroys civilisation, then attacks the few remaining humans to prevent them from deactivating it. In 1984 when the first *Terminator* film appeared, the most plausible strategy for Skynet to adopt is to start a nuclear war between the Cold War blocs. (Today there are many other ways a rogue super-AI could terminate humanity.) Doubtless the various movies and their time-travelling complexities are familiar enough to need no further elaboration here. The detail that Skynet is the US 'Global Digital Defense Network' created for its military by Cyberdyne Systems induces a frisson; there are numerous actual Cyberdynes producing AI military systems, and the 'What could possibly go wrong?' question asks itself more loudly every time one scrolls through the official website of DARPA (the US's Defense Advanced Research Projects

Agency). And that is just one place one can hear the question in the background; Silicon Valley and its analogues in other places are buzzing with hurry to make AI ever smarter, ever more competent, across as many domains as possible – a lot of it promising and good, yes, but too much of it making one wonder what would happen if it went wrong. The character Dyson says in *Terminator 2*, 'How were we supposed to know?' when the Schwarzenegger cyborg from the future (friendly in this film) tells him what his work will lead to. Today, we sort of do know.

One of the major aims of transhumanism as a project is to extend the period of human life. In the ideal the aim is to live forever. One way of doing the latter is to transfer mind and personhood to a platform, or a succession of platforms, that can preserve the continuity of the individual. The alternative of keeping a person's biological organism going so that it enjoys an active and healthy lifespan of, say, 150 years, is a more immediate aim, as presumably more realistic than transferring to a computer or machine. The non-biological version of longevity or immortality invites considerations different from biological life-extension, which are problematic in predictable ways – including such things as having to deal with a potential over-population problem by rationing babies, only some being permitted to have them, a situation exacerbated if 100-year-old women can still be fertile and desirous of having another child (and able to get, probably by being able to afford to buy it, a licence to do so).

Those wishing to prolong life significantly have not considered the sentiments of the three-centuries-old singer

Emilia Makropulos. She tells the men who want the longevity recipe she possesses that she has derived from her extended existence only exhaustion and a sense of futility, and that they should be happy because the prospect of death provides them with the opportunity to live and experience fully *because* of the knowledge that living and experiencing is limited. She cries out:

> One ought not, ought not, ought not to live so long! ... One can't go through with it. One lives for a hundred, or a hundred and thirty years, and then one realises – one finds out – that one's soul dies ... God! There is no word for it. Then one doesn't believe in anything. Not in anything! And from it comes that ennui. Berti, you used to say that I sang as if I were frozen. You see, art has meaning only so long as one doesn't understand; but when one understands all – one sees that singing is the same as keeping silent. Everything is the same. There is no difference in anything.

If biological life-lengthening happens through transhumanist interventions, but without enough in the way of support for the health and well-being of the long-livers, and without the economic transformation promised by an AI-run world, the impending disaster of Japanese demographics will occur. In 2025 the Japanese Health Ministry published figures showing that there are a hundred thousand centenarians in the country.[6] 'Japan now produces more nappies for incontinent adults than for infants. There is a burgeoning industry for the cleaning and fumigating of apartments in which elderly

Japanese citizens have died and been left undiscovered for weeks, months or years.[7] A growing number of elderly in most advanced economies, with fewer children being born per woman, is upending the age pyramid. Transhumanists envisage a world in which healthy, happy, robot-accompanied centenarian-plus people enjoy life, but what of the transition period? What if there is a mismatch in timing between longevity and the appropriate tech-created world they live in? And while transhumans are incompletely digitalised, what dissonances might there be between body and mind, and between both and the chips, electrodes, prosthetics of which they are partially constituted?

As the comment about 100-year-old women having babies implies, transhumanist enhancements are most probably only going to be available for some, not all, of humanity, at least for a time. Those who benefit, if fitter and better equipped with information and capabilities, will have advantages over those not enhanced. Today and in the foreseeable future the only people who can take advantage of enhancement are those with access to it – principally, those able to afford it for themselves and their offspring. This straight away initiates the process described by Huxley in *Brave New World* of a division in humanity, into superior and inferior classes of people.

In Huxley's novel this is achieved by incubating embryos in 'hatcheries' where they are modified, by the different chemical soups they develop in, into 'Alphas', 'Betas' and so on down to low-intelligence 'Epsilons', bred for menial labour. Sleep-conditioning indoctrination adapts them all to their roles. Two Alphas who visit a 'savage reservation' in New

Mexico, to see what naturally bred humans are like, are differently affected by the experience. One of them, a writer called Helmholtz, knows that his creativity is stifled by the insipid society of the Brave New World, whose denizens are kept quiescent by constant drinking of 'soma' which numbs them. He desires to be exiled to where dissidents are sent (as it happens, the Falkland Islands), hoping that living in and struggling with the harsh conditions there will kindle his creative imagination, and where in any case the world's most interesting people live because they do not fit into the Brave New World's system. Huxley is flagging the question one would ask of a society of healthy, contented people from whose existence much or all of the challenges of life as now lived have been lifted away. For Helmholtz, what gives meaning is the purpose found in endeavours to overcome, endure, seek among obstacles a path that is one's own.

In what way will transhumans have creativity-inspiring, some might add 'character-forming', challenges of the kind Helmholtz sought? In the ideal intention transhumans are to be free of the downsides afflicting natural humanity – anxiety, effort, disease, negative temptations, limitations of intellect and memory, emotional incapacities in one or another respect. Genetically modified and digitally enhanced, in this ideal they approach the condition of being bots, running on data. Perhaps transhumanists think of transhumans as retaining those features of humanity which, in their long lives, and although they are free of almost all kinds of suffering and difficulty that the natural human condition is beset by, still need what brings value to natural humanity, such as courage, continence, purpose, generosity, kindness. Yet it is hard to see why, given that they are programmed not to need them. Why will generosity and kindness be needed in a world where all are in clover? Why courage, in a world without threats or in beings without fear? Transhumanity would seem to be designed to negate the idea of essential selves, those loci of the experiences for which our best efforts to be our best selves require the concept of values, and which are the source of the sympathies that are the foundation of our best relationships. The more closely transhumans resemble bots, the further away they seem to be from essential selfhood.

The example of Aldous Huxley's Helmholtz accordingly prompts us to take seriously the thought that the concept of values applies chiefly, perhaps only, to essential selves. Of course, among the things humans value are peace of mind, leisure, ease, freedom from want, freedom from pain; contentment. These are principal eutopian aims for transhumanly modified beings in a seamlessly AI-run world. If their modifications, or AI-provided stimulations, make transhumans unsusceptible to the boredom that doing little or nothing brings to today's imperfect humans – what one feels in an over-long holiday in the same place, however pleasant the beach, the palm trees, the daiquiris at first – then the absence of challenge will not matter. But then the values of courage, continence, wisdom and justice will not matter either, because they will be otiose. In a perfected state of the eutopia implied, there will be no call for courage and wisdom, no call for generosity and kindness, because no occasion will require the first two, no one will need to be recipients of the second two.

Some kinds of love will remain, in whichever of its manifestations transhumanism regards as a positive rather than a negative. Remember that the ancient Greeks thought erotic love an infliction from the gods, because of the distractions of lust and the possibility of jealousy, hurt, loss, pain and grief as well as ecstasy – the last itself anyway transient. To put this kind of 'love' into a safe space, transhuman arrangements might include orgasmatrons such as feature in the films *Barbarella* and *Sleeper*; or perhaps bot companions will remove negative emotion from erotic passions, which anyway will only occur on one side of sexual encounters. Just as we can love our dogs and cats, we might love our chatbot partners, even though unlike dogs and cats there is no actual reciprocity of feeling – at very least of dependence or affiliation – such as dogs and cats give us. (I think dogs can be said to love their human companions in a quite literal acceptation of the term. But that perhaps is a dog-loving person's prejudice.) Indeed, 'loving your chatbot', given that there cannot be more than a simulacrum of return of love from a system that does not feel anything, raises a question. We say we love inanimate things like the countryside or that painting or this piece of music, but we are not using the word 'love' in the same way as lovers use the word to describe their attachment to each other, and this is the sense in which someone in a 'relationship' with a bot would be using (or, so to say, trying to use) the word. But the other half of the equation is missing: there is nothing there, no essential self, answering; there is only circuitry reacting to prompts. The more closely transhumans resemble bots in dispensing with the conditions of essential selfhood, the less even the idea of love has traction.

In an AI-run eutopia in which the AI systems lift away the burdens and remove the obstacles typical of human life as lived in the imperfect present, a feature will be the inverse relationship of AI power and human disempowerment. The more powerful and competent the AI, the less of either are humans, if only because they do not need to be. In an earlier chapter it was remarked that as specialisation in skills permeated human societies, so people lost all but the skills they needed to produce what they could exchange for the products of others' skills. AI systems are super-specialists, narrow AI in the applications they exist for, more general AI across much of the – or eventually the whole – board. In the latter case in particular, transhumans (or just humans, if AI runs the world before humans become fully transhuman) will need no skills.

In the current imperfect state of things we value our achievements. Some value learning. Some, making things; others, helping people. Each involves wrestling with a degree of resistance, overcoming which is the source of satisfaction. We enjoy leisure because we do not always have it. We enjoy being free of a burden because sometimes we carry burdens. Contrasts give the flavour to their opposites. Of course we do not wish to suffer greatly, nor (most of us) to see others suffer if there is anything we can do to help; the work of avoiding suffering – by making preparations, taking care of our health, managing our relationships productively, and so on – gives real point to these activities. The more ways that suffering is removed from our path, something we naturally all desire given that we experience too much of it for our liking, the less point there is to the related preventative and ameliorative activities attendant on it. That might be a very good thing as regards suffering; but what if the point is evacuated too much from the experience of being alive in other ways too – from the endeavour to meet challenges which AI and transhuman capabilities are designed to remove from our paths?

The thought that to *be* is to *do* – that the value of life is in its activities and aims, in how far we can get along the road to a desired destination, and in the small and large satisfactions of small and large achievements including staging-post ones – carries within it the thought that a too-perfect, too-easy, untroubled eutopia will *ipso facto* not be a eutopia, but a dystopia, as Huxley's Brave New World is, even for some of its Alphas. And then there is the thought that an AI-run society might be anything but a Brave New World, instead an Orwellian 1984, a surveillance society, a regimented, stipulative, monochrome society permanently gaslit, without freedom, without latitude. There is a minor version of this which is not 1984-ish in the sense of Big Brother watching, but where the gadget you wear on your wrist acts as a personal admonisher, nagger, insisting that you walk more steps or eat greens or switch off your laptop because your bedtime is due in an hour. The belief that it knows better than you what is good for you will be enough to make it a little Big Brother, reducing the autonomy of your life.

It is this last remark that brings us back full circle to the insistence that what we should take into the future from all humanity's past is our essential *human* selves, for they are the locus of autonomy, the place of choice, the subject to which most of the things we value pertain: the thing to which alone the ideas of courage, friendship, justice, purpose, experience and desire apply, all related to what constitutes, and derives from, relationships between essential selves, and only possible between essential selves. If one were the only human being left in a world of bots, very few of these values would have meaning, and those few only in the most residual and wholly self-directed sense. A natural human being who survives into a transhuman world would have a hard time relating to transhumans. An essential self has a biography, and in relationships between essential selves biographies impinge and have effects on each other. A bot does not have a biography, only a timeline. Interactions with it add to its data set, nothing else. In such an interaction an entire half of what gives rise to what we value is missing except as a nominal imitation of what there would be if another essential self were present. How far along the path to nominal selfhood would transhumans be in the ideal intention for transhumanity?

Another way of putting this point is to say that what we should take into the future is our capacity to choose how to be and act *because* what we are and how we act entangles with such choices made by genuine others. In real life – IRL – these entanglements can be as productive of strife and difficulty as positives, but even these are constitutive of both or all parties to the entanglements. To interact with a bot is to interact with what, on the other side of the mimic self – the nominal self – is a deep silence, a nothing. There is no one home there. We need to be told who or what will be at home in a being genetically and digitally enhanced beyond natural human character and the values it needs to live by to deal with its inadequacies.

Yet another way of putting the point is to say that if/when the AI-run transhumanised future comes, and if I am still alive then, *I* want to be there, and I want other '*I*'s to be there too. I want to be among genuine referents of the pronoun 'I', because almost everything of value in existence relates to what genuine referents of 'I' do, feel, and mean within themselves and in their relationships with other genuine referents of 'I'. At very best a bot could be indistinguishable on the surface from a genuine 'I', but until the day, if ever it comes, that an AI system is conscious and self-conscious, there is no deep noise of selfhood within, where *someone* is at home. If a transhuman is a bot in unblemished human skin, will he, she or it be at home in a way that an essential self could recognise?

And if there are 'I's in the future whose 'I-ness' has not been transhumanised away from feeling or needing the valued things – courage, kindness, purpose, desire – then these are the values, the *human* values, that *ipso facto* are to be taken forward along with them.

NOTES

All website links were correct as of 29 December 2025.

Introduction

1   A eutopia is a good place, a human paradise, the 'eu' prefix meaning 'good'.

1. 'Artificial' 'Intelligence'

1   Norbert Wiener, *The Human Use of Human Beings* (Houghton Mifflin, 1950); *Cybernetics* (MIT Press, rev. ed. 1961).
2   Nick Bostrom and Eliezer Yudkowsky, *The Cambridge Handbook of Artificial Intelligence* (Cambridge University Press, 2014), chapter 15.
3   Future of Life Institute (FLI), Open Letter, 28 July 2015: www.stopkillerrobots.org/wp-content/uploads/2013/03/FLI_LtrJuly2015.pdf.
4   Sebastian Herrera, 'Microsoft Lays Out Ambitious AI Vision, Free from OpenAI', *Wall Street Journal*, 6 November 2025: www.wsj.com/

tech/ai/microsoft-lays-out-ambitious-ai-vision-free-from-openai-297652ff. See Mustafa Suleyman, *The Coming Wave* (Bodley Head, 2023).

5   Robert Booth, '"The Biggest Decision Yet": Jared Kaplan on Allowing AI to Train Itself', *Guardian*, 3 December 2025: www. theguardian.com/technology/ng-interactive/2025/dec/02/ jared-kaplan-artificial-intelligence-train-itself.

6   Ibid.

7   Ibid.

8   Ibid.

9   Ibid.

10 Ibid.

11 US labour force in agriculture: US Census Bureau, 'Changes in Agriculture, 1900 to 1950': https://www2.census.gov/prod2/ decennial/documents/41667073v5p6ch4.pdf.

12 Frederick Jackson Turner, 'The Significance of the Frontier in American History', *The Frontier in American History* (H. Holt and Co., 1920), p. 293.

13 See 'Horses Lose Their Jobs', Wesley Living History Farm: https://livinghistoryfarm.org/farming-in-the-1940s/machines/ horses-lose-their-jobs/.

14 FLI, Open Letter, 22 October 2025: www.ddg.fr/actualite/ the-statement-on-superintelligence-by-the-future-of-life-insti-tute-october-2025-toward-a-conditional-ban-on-superintelli-gence-development.

15 EU AI Act, European Parliament, 8 June 2023: www.europarl. europa.eu/topics/en/article/20230601STO93804/eu-ai-act-first-regulation-on-artificial-intelligence.

16 Ibid.

17 FLI, Open Letter, 22 October 2025.

18 A. C. Grayling, *For the People* (Oneworld, 2025).

19 Daniel Susskind, *A World Without Work* (Allen Lane, 2020).

20 It is apposite to reference here an excellent article by Jonathan Haidt on social media and its effects: 'The Devil's Plan to Ruin the Next Generation', *The Free Press*, 25 November 2025: www.thefp.com/p/jonathan-haidt-the-devils-plan-to-ruin-next-generation.

21 Bas Fransen, 'The Climate Cost of Internet Data', *EcoMatcher*, 30 June 2025: www.ecomatcher.com/the-climate-cost-of-internet-data/.

22 Aaron Regunberg, 'Americans Hate AI. Will the Democrats Join Them?', *New Republic*, 12 November 2025: https://newrepublic.com/article/202878/ai-data-centers-democrats-election-wedge-issue. See also Gerrit de Vynck, 'The Surprising Issue Driving a Wedge between Trump and His MAGA Base', *Washington Post*, 23 November 2025: www.washingtonpost.com/technology/2025/11/23/trump-maga-division-tech-ai/.

2. Futures and Future People

1 Julian Huxley, 'Transhumanism', in *New Bottles for New Wine* (Chatto & Windus, 1957).

2 Ibid., pp. 13–14. I had not read Huxley before writing *The Frontiers of Knowledge* (Viking, 2021) but his allusions to the transformational effect of discoveries in history, biology, physics and psychology in the period since the mid-nineteenth century – this being the subject (with the exception of biology, Huxley's own specialism) of my account – strongly resonate with its premise.

3 Ibid., p. 16.

4 Ibid.

5 He does however mention in passing that 'dysgenic reproduction [could] reduce the average level of innate intellectual and moral qualities beyond a certain point' – a remark that should have struck a discord with him given the preceding half-century of eugenicist horrors. He is saved by two things: first, insisting that future evolutionary progress of humanity can only be cultural and social, not biological: natural selection will not operate on humans within the relevant time-frame, but will be a struggle 'between traditions and ideas, or between nations, classes, or other groups embodying those traditions and ideas' (ibid., p. 30); and second, by predicting that biological science (which includes medicine) will find ways of rectifying inherited problems so as to lift the heavy burden of suffering they impose (ibid., p. 306).

6 Ibid.

7 A summary and discussion of the Epic of Gilgamesh is given in my *Frontiers of Knowledge*.

8 See Nick Bostrom, 'A History of Transhumanist Thought', *Journal of Evolution and Technology*, Vol. 14 (April 2005): https://nick-bostrom.com/papers/a-history-of-transhumanist-thought/.

9 Leslie Bennetts, 'Among Futurists, a Prophet of Boom', *New York Times*, 11 July 1979.

10 FM-2030, *Are You a Transhuman?* (Warner Books, 1989), p. 201.

11 Ibid., p. 205.

12 Ibid., pp. 200–1.

13 Dr More was a pupil of mine at Oxford in the mid-1980s, and one of those whom I recommended for postgraduate study to the University of Southern California. It is very likely that we

discussed together Locke's theory of personal identity in *An Essay Concerning Human Understanding*, book II, chapter 27 (2nd ed., 1791). It cannot be coincidental that my colleague Jonathan Glover's *What Sort of People Should There Be?* (Penguin, 1984) appeared during More's time at Oxford; not long before my and More's time at St Anne's College I had substituted for Glover's sabbatical leave at New College, taking his classes and pupils, before then – while a doctoral student myself – attending his classes. Glover's book is another spur to transhumanist thinking, canvassing as it does human-transforming possibilities of genetics and technology. Aggregating Glover, More, Bostrom and others associated with Oxford, it would seem that the contemporary transhumanist movement could trace its proximal roots to that institution. Accordingly I should add that although I find many of the arguments interesting and indeed persuasive, I am not myself a member of the transhumanist movement, but an observer of it with an appreciation of some of its aspirations but concerns about how well it can guard itself against relapse by some of its advocates to positions against which the Nuremberg Code (1947) and the Declaration of Helsinki (1964) set themselves as barriers.

14 Bostrom, 'History', p. 12.

15 The *Declaration* appears in full as an appendix to ibid., pp. 21 *et seq.*

16 Ibid.

17 Julian Savulescu, 'Procreative Beneficence: Why We Should Select the Best Children', *Bioethics*, Vol. 15 (2001).

18 Ibid.

19 Aldous Huxley, *Brave New World* (Chatto & Windus, 1932).

20 I first enunciated this law, which I named after myself as an act of ownership for what is a dismaying predictive generalisation, in *For the Good of the World* (Oneworld, 2022).

21 See Dennis Normile, 'Chinese Scientist who Produced Genetically Altered Babies Sentenced to 3 Years in Jail', *Science*, 30 December 2019: www.science.org/content/article/chinese-scientist-who-produced-genetically-altered-babies-sentenced-3-years-jail.

22 James Hughes, 'The Politics of Human Enhancement Today', *Medium*, 8 July 2022: https://medium.com/institute-for-ethics-and-emerging-technologies/the-politics-of-human-enhancement-today-363ae71bf313.

23 Ibid.

24 Ibid.

25 See my *Discriminations* (Oneworld, 2025) which defends the underlying impulse to wokism, namely, opposition to discrimination in the forms of racism, sexism, homophobia, marginalisation of alternative gender and sexuality preferences – and, one might add, the aged and the disabled. Whereas I do not endorse some of the manifestations of more vigorous 'woke' activism, produced by frustration and anger at the continuation of discriminatory attitudes and practices, I see it as a chapter in the strong uptick of activity that began after the Second World War with civil rights and feminist claims to have the hitherto denied human rights of discriminated-against people respected.

26 Hughes, 'Politics'.

27 Ibid.

28 Elon Musk at a recorded Q&A, 'Elon Musk Says You Could Save and Replay Memories with Neuralink (Just Like Black Mirror)',

CNET Highlights, YouTube, 29 August 2020: www.youtube. com/watch?v=TrVKfRH_v3I.

29 Sam Altman, 'The Merge', 7 December 2017: https://blog.samalt-man.com/the-merge.

30 Aisha Down, 'Investors' "Dumb Transhumanist Ideas" Setting Back Neurotech Progress, Say Experts', *Guardian*, 10 November 2025: www.theguardian.com/science/2025/nov/10/investors-transhumanist-ideas-neurotech-progress-elon-musk.

31 John Carey (ed.), *The Faber Book of Utopias* (Faber and Faber, 2000), Introduction.

32 Ibid.

3. Space

1 In my *Who Owns the Moon?* (Oneworld, 2024) I set out the current commercially-driven race for the moon – more accurately: return to the moon – and, while acknowledging the positives that could flow from it, discuss the danger of space-race competition turning into conflict without a robust framework of agreements governing what happens in space.

2 *The Artemis Accords*, NASA: www.nasa.gov/wp-content/uploads/2022/11/Artemis-Accords-signed-13Oct2020.pdf.

3 This is discussed in Grayling, *Who Owns the Moon?*

4 Scepticism about the Artemis Accords is more fully stated in ibid.

5 Ibid.

6 Jean Fouré, Agnès Bénassy-Quéré and Lionel Fontagné, 'The World Economy in 2050: A Tentative Picture', CEPII working paper: www.cepii.fr/PDF_PUB/wp/2010/wp2010-27.pdf.

7   Chase Hamilton, 'Space and Existential Risk: The Need for Global Coordination and Caution in Space Development': https://scholarship.law.duke.edu/cgi/viewcontent.cgi?article=1372&context=dltr.

8   Ibid., pp. 34–5.

9   Ibid., p. 36.

10 Kim Stanley Robinson's *Mars Trilogy* provides some interesting indications of what any of this might look like, without straying too far from scientific realities. As regards an artificial space-station-type Earth: at time of writing a number of projects are in development for large advanced space stations by Gravitics, Blue Origin/Sierra, Northrop, Nanoracks/Airbus, Axiom, Vast and others, constituting steps on the road to possible permanent human-dwelling artificial colonies in space. That might not be the current intention, but lessons for doing it lie here.

11 These, and their relevance to space, are discussed in detail in Grayling, *Who Owns the Moon?*

12 Committee on the Peaceful Use of Outer Space, United Nations General Assembly, 64th Session, Vienna, May 2025, 'Initial Draft Set of Recommended Principles for Space Resource Activities': https://docs.un.org/en/A/AC.105/C.2/L.339.

13 Ibid.

14 The complicated and unresolved question of 'commons', 'province of all humankind' and associated ideas are discussed in full in Grayling, *Who Owns the Moon?*

15 See John Love, 'Monitoring Microorganisms', NASA, 18 January 2024: www.nasa.gov/missions/station/iss-research/monitoring-microorganisms/.

16 'Case Study: Fossil Microbes on Mars?', Cosmic Horizons Curriculum Collection, American Museum of Natural History: www.amnh.org/learn-teach/curriculum-collections/cosmic-horizons-book/fossil-microbes-mars.

4. The Climate

1 Alejandra Borunda, Jeff Brady, Michael Copley, Rebecca Hersher, Julia Simon and Lauren Sommer, 'Countries Are Gathering for Climate Negotiations. Here's Where the US Stands', NPR, 10 November 2025: www.npr.org/2025/11/10/nx-s1-5601876/trump-cop30-climate-brazil-belem.

2 'Unleashing American Energy', 20 January 2025: www.white house.gov/presidential-actions/2025/01/unleashing-american-energy/.

3 Laura Paddison, 'Welcome to the Planet's Newest Oil Frontier', CNN, 10 November 2025: https://edition.cnn.com/2025/11/10/climate/south-america-oil-gas-brazil-guyana-argentina-climate.

4 Echo Daily Flash, 10 November 2025: https://reliefweb.int/report/brazil/brazil-severe-weather-media-inmet-echo-daily-flash-10-november-2025.

5 'For the First Time, Climate Models Show the 1.5°C Goal is Dead', *The Economist*, 4 November 2025: www.economist.com/graphic-detail/2025/11/04/for-the-first-time-climate-models-show-the-15c-goal-is-dead.

6 Alison Withers and Stine Jacobsen, 'Iceland Deems Possible Atlantic Current Collapse a Security Risk', *Reuters*, 12 November 2025:www.reuters.com/sustainability/cop/iceland-sees-security-

risk-existential-threat-atlantic-ocean-currents-possible-2025-11-12/.

7   Attracta Mooney, 'The World Is Struggling to Halt Climate Change. But Can It Adapt?', *Financial Times*, 13 November 2025: www.ft.com/content/caf9895d-63b7-4410-969a-2cee059 10213.

8   Martin Sandbu, 'The Weakening Arctic Consensus Is Worrying', *Financial Times*, 20 April 2025: www.ft.com/content/20b4c69f-06d5-4c60-82b5-c0cf52b98f3d.

9   Ibid.

10 I discuss some of these in *For the Good of the World* (Oneworld, 2022).

11 'China's Clean-Energy Revolution Will Reshape Markets and Politics', *The Economist*, 6 November 2025: www.economist.com/leaders/2025/11/06/chinas-clean-energy-revolution-will-reshape-markets-and-politics.

12 'Net Zero by 2050 Too "Little Too Late"', Institute of Sustainability and Environmental Professionals: www.isepglobal.org/articles/net-zero-by-2050-too-little-too-late-scientists-warn.

13 Jyoti Thakur, 'On Super Hot Days, This Insurance Plan Pays Out Cash for Lost Wages', Goats and Soda, NPR, 16 July 2025: www.npr.org/sections/goats-and-soda/2025/07/16/g-s1-76948/hot-temperatures-insurance-gig-workers-india.

14 Luke Kemp *et al.*, 'Climate Endgame: Exploring Catastrophic Climate Change Scenarios', *Proceedings of the National Academy of Sciences*, 1 August 2022: https://doi.org/10.1073/pnas.2108146119.

15 Intergovernmental Panel on Climate Change (IPCC), *Climate Change 2022: Impacts, Adaptation and Vulnerability* (Cambridge

University Press, 2023), pp. 257–60: https://doi.org/10.1017/9781009325844.

16 Ibid.

17 Ibid.

18 Ibid.

19 Ibid.

20 Abigail E. Cahill *et al.*, 'How Does Climate Change Cause Extinction?', *Proceedings of the Royal Society B: Biological Sciences*, Vol. 280, No. 1750 (2013): https://royalsocietypublishing.org/doi/10.1098/rspb.2012.1890.

21 IPCC, *Climate Change 2022*.

22 David Stainforth, 'The Model of Catastrophe', *Aeon*, 11 November 2025: https://aeon.co/essays/todays-complex-climate-models-arent-equivalent-to-reality.

5. Coda

1 Quoted by Kaiser Kuo, 'The Great Reckoning: What the West Should Learn from China', *The Ideas Letter*, 16 October 2025: www.theideasletter.org/essay/the-great-reckoning/.

2 Ibid.

3 Adam Zeman's identification of the neurological condition of aphantasia has attracted international commendation. The name itself was provided by another friend – he, Zeman and I were students at Oxford together – the classicist and philosopher Professor David Mitchell of Northeastern University London.

6. Letting Go

1 I discuss the nature, history and ethics of war in *War: An Enquiry* (Yale University Press, 2017).

2 Ibid.

3 Ibid.

4 Ibid.

5 Ibid.

6 Joe Hasell, Bertha Rohenkohl, Pablo Arriagada, Esteban Ortiz-Ospina and Max Roser, 'Economic Inequality', Our World in Data, 2023: https://ourworldindata.org/economic-inequality.

7 Abhirup Roy and Akash Sriram, 'Elon Musk's $1 Trillion Tesla Pay Plan Wins Shareholder Approval', *Reuters*, 7 November 2025: www.reuters.com/legal/transactional/tesla-shareholders-approve-878-billion-pay-plan-elon-musk-2025-11-06/.

8 More detail on all these matters is to be found in my *For the People*.

9 See Sharjeel Tareef, 'Scandinavia's Social Model: Lessons from a High-Tax, High-Welfare Success Story', *Friday Times*, 28 May 2025: www.thefridaytimes.com/28-May-2025/scandinavia-s-social-model-lessons-from-a-high-tax-high-welfare-success-story.

10 'Justice', Legal Information Institute, Cornell Law School: www.law.cornell.edu/wex/justice#:~:text=Justice%20is%20the%20ethical%2C%20philosophical,and%20the%20accused%20receive%20a.

11 I. Barberis *et al.*, 'The History of Tuberculosis: from the First Historical Records to the Isolation of Koch's Bacillus', *Journal of Preventive Medicine and Hygiene*, Vol. 58, No. 1 (2017): https://pmc.ncbi.nlm.nih.gov/articles/PMC5432783/.

12 'Flu (Influenza)', Mayo Clinic, www.mayoclinic.org/diseases-conditions/history-disease-outbreaks-vaccine-timeline/flu.

13 This is the insistent theme of my *Discriminations* (Oneworld, 2025), where the case for it is set out in full.

7. The Idea of Values

1 Reading scores of novels as a Booker Prize judge in 2003 and 2014 I was struck by how much they collectively portrayed the times, all of them being contemporary to the times, and yet how perennial the experiential themes in them were.

2 See my *Philosophy and Life* (Viking, 2023), chapter 5 *passim.*

3 Ibid., especially chapter 6.

4 The term 'axial age' was introduced by Karl Jaspers to denote the great change in thinking that occurred between the eighth and fourth centuries BCE in all the ancient civilisations, most notably in Greece, India and China, though Jaspers included the Judaic and Persian civilisations also. A more focused account of this revolution, predicated on distinguishing philosophical from religious thought, is given by the present writer in a forthcoming volume to be published by Transworld in 2027.

5 Grayling, *Philosophy and Life*, chapter 4.

8. Utopia

1 Ursula Le Guin, 'The Ones Who Walk Away from Omelas', in *The Wind's Twelve Quarters* (Harper & Row, 1975).

2   This is the inspiration for David Graeber and David Wengrow, *The Dawn of Everything* (Penguin, 2021).

3   See my *The Age of Genius* (Bloomsbury, 2016).

4   Robert Boyle, the father of chemistry, likewise; he was scammed into parting with a large sum in return for alchemical secrets allegedly available in Turkey. See ibid.

5   See my *Descartes* (Simon and Schuster, 2005).

6   Quoted by W. D. Armes in his introduction to *The Utopia* (Macmillan, 1912).

7   It is remarkable how thin is the tissue between socialist economics and fascist social policy, as evidenced in this imagined application of theory and in twentieth-century history's facts. To one who is, like the present writer, a social democrat, on the small-l liberal Left in politics and economics though considerably further left on social policy (as a supporter of important aspects of what underlies so-called 'woke' issues), it comes as a surprise to find this position so revolutionary to hold, given the contempt in which it is held both by the Right (everyone there) and by the far Left. And yet the moderate Left is arguably the sweet spot where civil liberties and social justice have most chance of existing together.

8   See Peter S. Goodman, Will Fitzgibbon, Melanie Bencosme, Finbarr O'Reilly, Jon Miller, June Kim, Laura Salaberry and Carmen Abd Ali, 'The Real Cost of US Car Batteries', *New York Times*, 18 November 2025: www.nytimes.com/video/world/africa/100000010500077/the-real-cost-of-us-car-batteries.html.

9. Back to the Future

1   See Robert Booth, 'ChatGPT Firm Blames Boy's Suicide on "Misuse" of Its Technology', *Guardian*, 26 November 2025: www.theguardian.com/technology/2025/nov/26/chatgpt-openai-blame-technology-misuse-california-boy-suicide.

2   To pre-empt one kind of objection to the concept of the self I outline, note that nothing metaphysical is implied; I mean empirically-experienced subjectivity as a continuing locus of experience from the position of which in space and time the objects and sources of that experience are viewed – and, most importantly, *felt*.

3   See Gil Press, 'AI Companion Robot Says Hello to Japan's 36 Million Seniors', *Forbes*, 8 September 2025: www.forbes.com/sites/gilpress/2025/09/08/ai-companion-robot-says-hello-to-japans-36-million-seniors/.

4   Ibid.

5   See Alyssa Hui-Anderson, 'What Is "Bed Rotting"? Gen Z's Newest Self-Care Trend, Explained', health.com, 2 August 2025: www.health.com/what-is-bed-rotting-trend-7561395.

6   David Runciman, 'Are We Doomed?', *London Review of Books*, 20 November 2025: www.lrb.co.uk/the-paper/v47/n21/david-runciman/are-we-doomed.

7   Ibid.

INDEX